1964

Merry C...
to Cha...
from Dad & Mom

38
8F

Indian Ocean Treasure

Arthur C. Clarke

INDIAN OCEAN

Illustrated with

Harper & Row, Publishers

and Mike Wilson

TREASURE

photographs and maps

New York, Evanston and London

All photographs not otherwise credited were taken by Mike Wilson.

To Mark and Bobby

Contents

x

Acknowledgments

Among the many people and institutions who assisted us in this project, we would especially like to thank:

    Peter Throckmorton, who abandoned his own work at a moment's notice to join us.

    Frank Rees, O.B.E., and his successor, Lieutenant

Commander E. W. de la Mare, R.N.R., of the Imperial Lighthouse Service, for the hospitality of the Great Basses lighthouse.

The Avon Rubber Company for their gift of two REDSHANK dinghies, without which operations on the reef would have been impossible.

Colin McLeod, of Messrs. Lillywhites, London, for assistance with equipment.

Montres Rolex, SA, Geneva, for underwater watches.

Mendel Peterson, of the Smithsonian Institution, for his technical advice.

The Imperial Lighthouse staff at Kirinda for good-naturedly sharing their accommodations with us.

Major R. Raven-Hart, and the ladies of Writer's & Speaker's Research, London, for much digging into dusty archives.

Dr. C. E. Godakumbure, and the staff of the Department of Archaeology, Colombo, Ceylon, for co-operating with us in the investigation and protection of this unique site.

A.C.C.

M.W.

1. Of Time and Treasure

Sunken treasure!

No pair of words in the language holds more magic; for who has not dreamed, at some time or other, of diving into one of the lost galleons of the Spanish Main, loaded with its precious cargo of gold and silver? Millions—no, *billions*—of dollars' worth of treasure lies at the bottom of the sea, buried beneath the coral of centuries. And it is rare indeed for any to be found; for the sea is enormous—three times larger than all the land, and much more difficult to explore.

When treasure is found, it is almost always by accident. There is a very good reason for this, though it is surprising how often it is overlooked. In the past whenever a cargo of treasure was lost at a *known* spot, attempts were naturally made at once to recover it. Because it has made such great strides in this century, we often think that diving is a modern achievement—but of course it is not. For thousands of years there have been men who could do active work at depths of a hundred feet or more, staying under water for two or three minutes. Whenever a valuable cargo went down in reasonably shallow water, divers were quickly called in; and they usually did a very good job. Most of the great treasure wrecks of the past were promptly salvaged, and only their scattered timbers were left on the sea bed when the divers had finished their work.

Of course there are plenty of exceptions to this, but on the whole it is true to say that a treasure ship that everybody knew about at the time of its loss no longer holds any treasure. The ships that *still* hold treasure are those that sank in water too deep for salvage work or were lost at sea without survivors, so that no man knows their graves.

Such a ship may lie in quite shallow water, perhaps even awash on some lonely reef. After a few seasons the waves will smash it to pieces and scatter its cargo far and wide. For a year or two the sea bed may be carpeted with gold and silver—a fortune lying to be picked up by anyone who can hold his breath for fifteen seconds. This must have happened scores of times along the great treasure routes of the past.

But the treasure will lie glittering in the open for only a very few years; soon the heavy gold will work itself into the sea bed, and the silver will start to corrode. And all the while mud and sand will be sweeping over the wreck, or, if it is in the tropics, the busy corals will be building their homes over every square inch of exposed surface. Within fifty years a diver might swim above the wreck and see nothing at all. Within a century everything will lie beneath yards of mud, or be sealed within a blanket of coral a foot thick and as hard as concrete.

Against such odds, the discovery of an old treasure wreck is almost a miracle. But miracles sometimes happen, especially to people who are ready for them.

This is how it happened to us.

2. The Great Reef

The story begins in 1958, two years after my partner, Mike Wilson, and I had settled down in Ceylon, following our first underwater expedition to that island (see *The Reefs of Taprobane*). During those two years we had done very little diving, as we had both been caught

4

up with lecture tours of the United States, which kept us away from our tropical home for months at a time.

Then Mike discovered some brand-new underwater territory, so spectacular and so unusual that it revived our interest in serious skin diving and submarine photography. This was the Great Basses Reef—a wave-swept line of submerged rocks, running parallel to the south coast of Ceylon at a distance of about six miles from the mainland. The curious name Basses comes from the Portuguese word for reef or shoal, *baixos,* so Great Basses simply means Great Reef.

Though it was dangerous and hard to get at, the reef looked promising because being so far from land, it would have very clear water—and its inhabitants would be un-afraid of man, for they would never have been hunted. More important still, it was possible to live on the reef, despite the fact that only a few patches of rock were above sea level, and even these were continually swept by waves. Ninety years ago, to protect the ships that are continually passing along this major trade route, the British Govern-ment built a great lighthouse here. Its construction on these remote and dangerous rocks was a wonderful feat of engineering. The whole lighthouse was first carved and assembled in Scotland, the two-ton blocks of granite were shipped out to Ceylon, and the 110-foot-high tower was erected in only two hundred working days, without

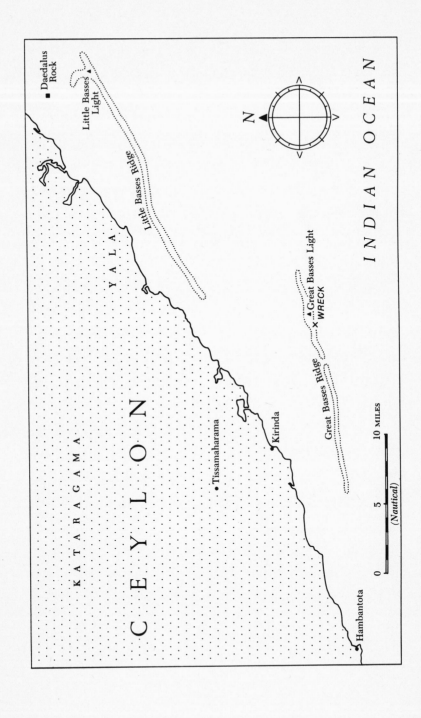

Daedalus
Rock ■

Little Basses
Light ▲

Little Basses Ridge

KATARAGAMA

YALA

CEYLON

Tissamaharama •

Kirinda •

Great Basses Light ▲
× WRECK

Great Basses Ridge

INDIAN OCEAN

N

Hambantota •

0   5   10 MILES

(Nautical)

any injuries or loss of life. To me this is quite incredible—and you may agree when you see some of the photographs in this book.

Thanks to the courtesy of the Imperial Lighthouse Service, we were able to use the lighthouse as our home, sharing it with the four keepers who are always on duty there. It was a strange, rugged, and exhausting life, which I have described in *Indian Ocean Adventure,* so here I will give only a brief summary of our first expeditions to the reef.

On his 1958 visit Mike was accompanied by Rodney Jonklaas, the Ceylonese diver-naturalist who first introduced us to the underwater beauties of the island. Mike and Rodney came back so full of enthusiasm that I decided to join them next time—even though some of the tales they told were quite hair-raising.

At this point I should explain that one can get near the Great Basses Reef for only a short period every year. For almost ten months out of the twelve the weather is so rough that it is impossible to approach the lighthouse; it is surrounded by boiling foam. Even in calm weather I have felt the tower vibrate beneath me like a giant tuning fork as the sea thunders against its foundations.

Fortunately the good weather can be predicted with a fair degree of accuracy. This is because the Indian Ocean has a mysteriously regular system of winds—the famous

The Great Basses Reef. Shark's Tooth Rock visible above the breakers on far right. ROYAL CEYLON AIR FORCE

monsoons—which come and go almost according to the calendar. From October to March the wind blows from the northeast; then it slackens, and there are about two months of calm weather. But between April and May the wind switches to the other direction; the southwest monsoon sets in, with heavy rain and violent storms. The only time that operations on the reef are possible, therefore, is through March and April; and we could not always count on this, for even the monsoon is not absolutely reliable.

9

The Great Basses lighthouse, photographed one month after the 1963 expedition. The wreck site is a quarter of a mile to the left.
ROYAL CEYLON AIR FORCE

A new crew for the lighthouse.

But in 1959 we were lucky; Mike, Rodney, and I spent a week on the reef in perfect weather. We were taken out, with the lighthouse stores and crew replacements, in the relief boat, which anchored about fifty feet away from the rocks. A thick rope was slung across to us from a crane on the lighthouse, and we were hauled up it, swinging back and forth, with our feet just above the waves. Up that same rope, a little later, went all our equipment— Aqua-Lungs, air compressor, underwater cameras, films, food—everything that would be needed for an expedition that would be completely cut off from the outside world until the relief boat appeared again. If we were unlucky, that might not be for weeks.

Then followed the hardest work I have ever done (or perhaps ever will do) in my life. Merely living in the lighthouse was exhausting: the temperature was never less than ninety degrees, and we had to keep climbing up and down a spiral stairway a hundred feet high as we moved from one room to another. And this was merely the background to our real work, the diving.

But it was worth it. Around the lighthouse was a fantastic submarine fairyland of caves, grottoes, coral-encrusted valleys—and fish in numbers such as I have never met anywhere else in the world. Sometimes they crowded round us so closely that we could see nothing but a solid wall of scales and had literally to push our way through. They were inquisitive and completely unafraid. During our visit we met eagle rays, turtles, angelfish, jacks, tuna (up to three hundred pounds!), groupers, and sharks. Especially the latter.

One of Mike's chief objects in going to the reef had been to get some good shark pictures. We had encountered sharks scores of times in the past, but had never taken any really good photographs of them—they were always too shy. We hoped that the ocean-going sharks out here on the reef would be a little less nervous. This proved to be the case; by the time we had finished, *we* were the nervous ones. But Mike got his pictures, including a remarkable movie sequence of a determined attack on Rodney by a shark trying to grab a fish he was holding in his hand.

Rodney and author on the Great Basses Reef, preparing to dive off the edge.

A rough day on the reef; photographed from sea level on the light-house.

We spent most of our time, however, with a family of three giant groupers (jewfish) which Mike and Rodney had befriended and photographed the year before. As all skin divers know, groupers are large, intelligent, and fearless fish that will quickly attach themselves to you if you refrain from sticking spears into them and will become extremely friendly if you feed them, as we did. Ali Baba, Sinbad, and Aladdin would follow us around like tame dogs, waiting for tidbits, and eventually Rodney was able to make them carry out circus tricks such as swimming through hoops and taking food gently from his fingers. These, remember, were wild, flesh-eating animals—per-

13

A hungry shark tries to get at Rodney's fish.

haps the equivalent of bears or lions on land—whom we
had met only a few times over a period of a year.

Mike made a fine color movie, *Beneath the Seas of
Ceylon,* out of all this, and we departed quite satisfied
when the lighthouse relief boat called for us and took us
back to civilization at the end of the week. (Luckily for
Mike: a few days later, he had to be operated on for acute
appendicitis!) We had been so busy photographing the
groupers, sharks, and other local inhabitants that we had
done practically no sight-seeing and had certainly not gone

looking for wrecks, though we knew that there must be many in such a dangerous area. We would have laughed incredulously as we sailed back to the mainland, with the storm clouds of the southwest monsoon already gathering on the horizon behind us, if anyone had told us that all the while we had been within half a mile of treasure.

Just before we left I snapped Mike on the gallery of the lighthouse, a hundred feet above the sea, looking out thoughtfully across the reef. The result was a good portrait of the reef, though a poor one of Mike; and by a strange coincidence he was looking directly at the site of the treasure wreck, which he was not to discover until two years later, or to explore thoroughly until another four.

We missed 1960 because Mike spent the good diving

Mike on the lighthouse gallery, showing complete vista of the reef and the wreck site. Shark's Tooth Rock at center. ARTHUR CLARKE

season in the jungles of Borneo, taking color photographs for *Time* magazine. And when he returned to the Great Basses in 1961, neither Rodney nor I went with him.

Rodney was away on an underwater survey of the Maldive Islands, four hundred miles to the west of Ceylon; it was here that he made the interesting discovery that when you are diving at night, there are some sharks that will charge straight down the beam of your flashlight. For my part, I had decided that I was now too old and too fond of comfortable living for the rugged sort of existence one had to lead on the reef. I was very glad that I'd been there, but had no intention of risking my neck again on those barnacle-covered rocks.

In any case Mike managed very well without us. He took with him two young Americans who were first-class swimmers and divers. And when I say young, I mean it. Bobby Kriegel was fourteen and Mark Smith only thirteen. How Mike had managed to persuade their parents—members of the official U.S. community in Ceylon—to let the boys accompany him on such an expedition, I'll never know.

But he had it all worked out. He had decided to film an underwater fantasy about a little boy—Mark—who dreams that he's exploring the sea—and wakes up to find that his dream has come true. Mike had written a script not only for Mark, but also for Ali Baba, Sinbad, and

Aladdin. He was quite confident that they would still be in their cave and would do just what he told them when he arrived back on the scene with his cameras after a two-year absence.

Mark and Bobby were practically amphibians; they spent all their spare time in the water. We would often meet them cycling down to the sea, with their spearfishing gear tied to their bicycles, and see them coming back with fish draped across their handlebars. They were a complete contrast: Mark was very small-built and blond, looking much younger than his thirteen years, while Bobby was big and husky. And whereas Mark was an only child, Bobby was one of a large and handsome family that never stayed still long enough to be counted.

However, both were remarkably mature for their years and were extremely anxious to use the Aqua-Lung. On their very first lesson in the local swimming pool they were able to throw all their equipment—masks, fins, weight belt and Aqua-Lung—into the water, dive down, and put it all on again before coming to the surface.

They talked very little, but when they did say something, it was always constructive. By this I don't mean that they were solemn and serious—indeed, they were full of high spirits—but they realized that diving requires care and concentration. After a very few lessons Mike was confident that they could tackle all ordinary underwater jobs quite safely and wouldn't lose their heads in an emergency.

The three explorers set off from Colombo in our Volkswagen Microbus loaded with diving gear, and that was the last we heard of them for almost two weeks, except for a brief "All well" message flashed one night by Morse from the lighthouse. There was no telephone from Colombo to the tiny fishing village, 160 miles away, that is the jumping-off spot for the lighthouse, so we did not expect any real news of the expedition until it returned.

It was a great relief to everybody when, late one afternoon, Mike and the boys arrived back safely and started unloading the bus. When I asked them eagerly, "Well, how did it go?" they wouldn't give a straight answer, but mumbled something like, "Oh, not so badly," as they staggered into my office carrying a battered tin trunk.

On the outward trip, that trunk had contained our cameras. It seemed much heavier now, but I thought nothing of it until Mike locked the office door and said mysteriously, "Look at this."

He threw open the lid—and there were two beautiful little brass cannons, badly worn but gleaming brilliantly where the sea had polished them, and obviously very old. I cried out in excitement, "You've found an old wreck!" Like all divers, we'd been dreaming of this for years, but had never taken the idea very seriously.

18

Mark Smith (left) and Bobby Kriegel on the steps of the light-house platform.

Then, without saying a word, Mike lifted the guns and showed me what lay underneath them. At first I thought I was looking at dirty lumps of coral, about the size of coconuts. Then I realized just what those lumps were; and I was too astonished to say anything.

It was one of the unforgettable moments of a lifetime, for I knew then that I was staring at something very few men have ever seen—genuine, honest-to-goodness treasure. These unimpressive-looking lumps were masses of coins—hundreds of them, cemented together. When I bent down to pick one up, I could hardly lift it. It was not—alas!—heavy enough for gold; but it could only be the next best thing: silver.

Besides these big lumps there were hundreds of loose coins. Many were badly corroded, but most of them seemed to be in remarkably good condition. They were covered with what appeared to be Arabic or Persian lettering, and the total weight of silver came to about 115 pounds. "But," said Mike, "there's a lot more where we found this. . . ."

In addition to the coins and the little cannons, the expedition had recovered some small copper bars and about twenty lead musketballs. Altogether the salvaged material weighed about two hundred pounds, and it was an astonishing feat to have recovered it from the sea bed, got it safely to the lighthouse, then to the relief boat and across

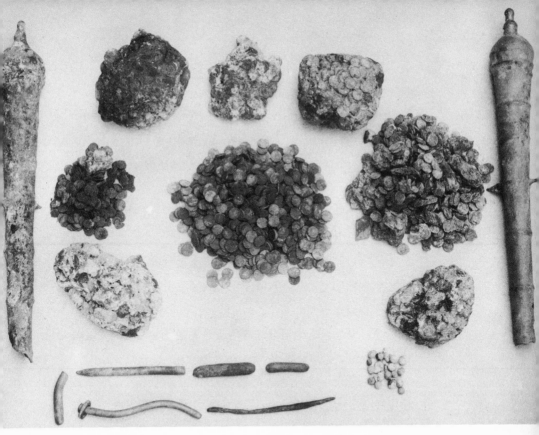

All the 1961 finds. The coin mass at upper right is now in the Smithsonian Institution, Washington, D.C.

ten miles of sea, and finally unloaded it on land—all without anyone seeing it.

That evening we asked the boys' parents around to our house; at our request, Mark and Bobby had not breathed a word about the discovery, though this must have been something of a strain. Then we had the pleasure of watching the Smiths and the Kriegels do a double take, exactly as I had done, when they looked into the treasure box and realized just what it held. During the next few days we were to grow accustomed to watching perplexity, wonder, disbelief, and finally excitement spread across the faces of the few trusted friends we introduced to the finds, which now rested safely in a massive wooden chest with a big brass padlock.

The first night the treasure reposed in our house I did not sleep at all soundly; I kept dreaming about burglars, and at 4:30 in the morning decided to get up and make myself a cup of tea. This disturbed Mike—who had been having similar dreams—and he emerged from his bedroom with his beloved Luger pistol at the ready. So we had a predawn conference, discussing what should be done; for we realized that something had happened that would change both our lives. The hundredweight of silver that lay in my office, though it was quite valuable, was only a sample. But where had it come from, whither was it bound, and how had it arrived at the bottom of the sea? These were only a few of the questions we had to answer; it was just as well that we could not get back to the reef for another year, for there were months of research ahead of us.

And it was also just as well that we did not know how many disappointments, frustrations, and disasters still lay ahead before either of us would see again the white tower of the Great Basses lighthouse standing guard over the treasure that the reef had held so long.

3. The Finding of the Treasure

The other day I came across Mark Smith's diary of the expedition; it is so brief and so tantalizing that I'd like to quote it in full. The first entry says simply: "March 12, 1961. Arrived."

That one word covers a 175-mile drive down the beautiful, palm-fringed, southwest coast of Ceylon—surely one of the loveliest in the world—past dozens of fishing villages with their picturesque outrigger boats drawn up on the beaches. The journey goes through the ancient port of Galle—which, say some historians, may be the Tarshish of the Bible—and beyond that into a lonely landscape of still lagoons and patches of jungle. You may meet wild elephants here, but they seldom bother motorists.

The end of the line, and the jumping-off point for the reef, is the little fishing village of Kirinda, situated on a wide, sweeping bay which gives no shelter at all when the monsoon gales blow. The Imperial Lighthouse Service has its boathouse here, a large shed high up on the beach, which normally houses the motor launch *Pharos*. Mike and the boys unloaded all their equipment here, and by the time they had finished this, Mark had no energy left for keeping a diary. By next morning, however, he'd recovered.

March 13. Surfed all day. In late afternoon repacked gear.

They went to bed early that night, because the *Pharos* would leave at the horrible hour of 4 A.M., when the sea was at its calmest. The ten-mile journey to the lighthouse, the giddy trip up the swaying rope, and the transfer of tons of equipment from pitching boat to the spray-

Too rough for diving!

drenched rocks at the base of the great tower, Mark sums up as follows:

March 14. Left for G.B. Stowed gear, etc.

Having been through all this myself, I am not in the least surprised that he had no energy to write any more; setting up house in a building one hundred feet high is one of the most exhausting jobs I know. But by the next morning operations were in full swing, and Mark becomes positively garrulous. I'll give the rest of his diary without a break:

March 15. Sea bad, strong current, big chop. No SCUBA

Mark Smith and Ali Baba.

diving, snorkled. Met Sinbad and Ali Baba, re-
gained friendship.

*March 16. Took first SCUBA dive. Saw and filmed group-
ers, Mike saw barracuda, big shark.*

March 17. Sea good, took two dives.

   1st. Filmed Sinbad and Ali Baba.

   *2nd. Saw dozen tunas, from 75 to 200 pounds.
Had big giant grouper (300 pounds) chase us.
Took stills of caves, batfish and groupers. Bobby
saw same (?) big shark as seen yesterday (10 ft.)*

Mark Smith coaxes Ali Baba through the hula hoop.

I think you'll agree that this is not a bad beginning for the expedition; but after that things got too hectic for Mark to continue his literary activities. Fortunately we have a full account of what happened next, for as soon as they returned to the mainland I interviewed both boys with a tape recorder while their impressions were still sharp and clear. So in what follows I am able to give their actual words, spoken while they were still gripped by the excitement of discovery.

Bobby Kriegel carries the Bolex movie camera to the "studio."

For the next four days, they continued diving and fishing. They would jump off the rugged, barnacle-encrusted edge of the reef and swim out to the groupers' home, about a hundred yards away, towing a large inflated inner tube from which the Aqua-Lungs and cameras were

Mark Smith carrying the Beaulieu underwater movie camera.

hung. If the currents were against them, this could be very hard work; it sometimes took half an hour to cover this short distance.

After anchoring the float, they would put on their lungs and dive down to the bottom, where the groupers would at once greet them with open mouths. Sometimes, if they were not fed immediately, they would become impatient, and on one occasion a greedy Sinbad swallowed Mark's arm up to the elbow. As the grouper was more than twice his size, there was nothing that Mark could do but wait until he got his arm back. Fortunately groupers have very small teeth, and the incident left only a few scars which Mark displayed proudly until they healed. Perhaps it was lucky that nothing like this happened with the *really* big grouper seen on March 17—an unfriendly character who was left strictly alone.

Then, on March 22—but let Bobby Kriegel tell you the story in his own words, as I took them down on the tape recorder:

Well, the sea was unusually calm; it fact, it was so calm that there was no current to take away the sand in the water. So it wasn't very clear and we couldn't get any pictures. That day some porpoises came unusually close, about fifty feet away from the lighthouse, and Mike, Mark, and I set off to see how close we could get to them. We saw them, and when they disappeared, we went away. Since there was no tide and we couldn't take any pictures, we decided to go down and explore one of the reefs which had never been seen underwater. So we went down there, and on the way, Mike told us later, he thought he saw a cannonball. Then we saw a small cannon, about two and

Mark Smith and Bobby Kriegel (left, carrying Rolleimarine under-water camera) swimming over the reef.

Mark Smith explores a cave on the Great Basses Reef.

a half feet long. Mike dived down—no, Mike didn't dive down to it. He showed it to me and pointed. I dived down and tried to pull it up. I couldn't do it. So then Mike dived down and lifted it free, then put it back down. Mike said that the wreck might have hit on one side of the reef and some more might be on the other side; so we swam around the edge of it.

After we got to the other side, the first thing we saw was a shiny cannon, about two and a half feet long, sitting on the edge of a big canyon; and it was worn smooth by the water, and shining as though someone had put it there the other day.

These two little cannons (their correct name is "swivel guns") had been polished by the waves and sand until their brass gleamed like gold. From a distance, indeed,

Close-up of swivel-gun breech, showing ornamentation.

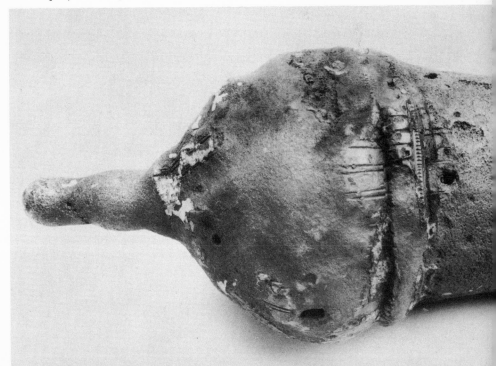

they looked brand-new. They were the unmistakable sign-posts without which the wreck might never have been discovered. We think now that they must have been well up on the tall stern of the ship and fell on the higher part of the reef when she went aground. They had been lying there for centuries, rolling back and forth in the swell which surges almost continually across the reef in bad weather and in good.

It is nearly always cannons that betray an old wreck. When the hull decays and collapses, which takes only a few years, cannons remain intact. Even when they have become completely covered with coral, their straight lines are an immediate giveaway, for nothing natural in the sea is perfectly straight.

But back to Mike and the boys. . . .

They were a long way from the lighthouse—more than a thousand feet, which is a tremendous distance to cover, even for a good swimmer, against the powerful currents that sweep along the reef. Also they had no Aqua-Lungs and no underwater cameras, for, after all, they had merely been on a sight-seeing trip. So they decided that the best thing to do was to go back to the lighthouse, have lunch, and return properly equipped in the afternoon.

After a hasty meal they were back on the site with their Aqua-Lungs and the big inner tube. Now they were able to make a more thorough investigation, and slowly

34

the pattern of the wreck began to emerge. The hull had been smashed to pieces, and no trace of it was left. In fact, ninety-nine out of a hundred skin divers would have swum right over the site without seeing a thing—except for one cannon, about five feet long, which lay on the sea bed like a fallen column from some Greek temple. Not far from it were shapeless mounds which, on more careful inspection, turned out to be two huge anchors tangled together. And near what must have been the middle of the ship was a pile of about a dozen iron cannons, jumbled together like matchsticks spilled from a box.

It was that afternoon, on their second dive, that they made the big discovery that turned this from another old wreck to something even more exciting. Listen to Mark Smith's rather breathless account, which I think conveys the drama of that moment very well:

We took out the big inner tube and were going to take out the filming equipment, but Bob drifted down the current so fast that Mike put the film equipment away and we went out with Aqua-Lungs. Then, when we got near the spot, we turned on our Aqua-Lungs and went down and Mike was hitting everything he saw with his knife. Then Mike came over to us and showed us the cannon, and Bob pointed out something shining right near it. Mike examined it and said it was silver—underwater with his mouthpiece on!

Both boys were much impressed by this last feat. It's normally impossible to talk underwater when you are gripping an Aqua-Lung mouthpiece between your teeth, but Mike yelled "Silver!" so loudly that they both heard him.

Then the hunt was on. Listen to Mark again:

Then we all three started to uncover the sand. We pushed it away and then we saw all the coins stuck to the rock. So

Bobby Kriegel lifts one of the coin masses. Even under water the thirty-pound lump is hard to handle. This may be the first photo ever taken showing sunken treasure at the moment of recovery.

we started working on the coins and that day we got a small bagful of loose coins and a few little pieces of coral with coins in it. Then we took it back to the lighthouse at the time that the lighthouse keepers were taking a nap. . . .

Already the little expedition was up against the problem that would give us one of our biggest headaches in the future—security. They could not guess the importance of this find, but it was obviously wise to keep it secret for the present. There were four lighthousemen with them on the rock, and if the news got back to land, there was always a possibility that someone else might come out and clean up the wreck. They were not the only divers in Ceylon.

Mark continues:

We spread all the treasure out and the two cannons that we'd got, and Mike photographed them. We put the silver inside a kit bag, but we didn't show the lighthouse keepers the treasure, though we showed them the two cannons that we'd got. The next day, early morning, the water was still not clear around the lighthouse, so we went out to the wreck—this time with all the equipment: knives, crowbars, and chisels, and the big inner tube. This time we also took the still cameras. We went off to the place and this time we got a lot of bags full of loose coins and some chunks of silver coins. Then we went back to the

Bobby Kriegel (top) and Mark Smith with their finds on the Great Basses lighthouse, photographed on the day of the discovery of the wreck (March 22, 1961).

lighthouse, and that afternoon we spent our time chipping out the coins and washing them. The next morning we went out and got the big hunks of silver coins—four big lumps and some loose ones. And that was the last time we went out to the wreck; we paddled back to the lighthouse and squared everything away. . . .

The underwater photographs that Mike took on these two trips are, as far as I know, the only ones ever made showing treasure at the actual moment of recovery from the sea bed. We have kept them secret for over two years, but we do not mind publishing them now; for this section of the reef looks quite different today, thanks to the hard work done by our latest expedition.

Altogether, Mike and the boys spent only two days diving on the wreck, without proper equipment and with no boat. Yet they brought back some two hundred pounds of material, including the two little swivel guns, which weigh about thirty pounds each. As the swim to the lighthouse often took more than an hour, this was a really astonishing performance. Now that I have visited the site myself, I am still more amazed at what they accomplished.

Then the water became clear again, and they continued with the movie-making—which is what they had come to do in the first place. Mike took the final shots of his fantasy, showing Mark swimming slowly through the

Mike examines the treasure; lighthouse crane in background.
BOBBY KRIEGEL

blue-green valleys of the reef while Sinbad, Aladdin, and Ali Baba escort him like three friendly dogs. Mark turns to wave good-by to them as they drop behind. To us now, that gesture has a special poignancy, for none of us would

40

ever see the groupers again. That was the end of our three-year partnership.

The next year some foreign "sportsmen" who had seen Mike's movies and stills and had heard rumors of the treasure went out to the reef. They had no difficulty, of course, in spearing Sinbad, Ali Baba, and Aladdin when they swam up to them trustfully, expecting to be fed.

But at least the brave hunters did not find the wreck.

4. Mogul Silver

The first order of business was, clearly, the identification of the coins. When we had cleaned the loose ones in battery acid, which dissolved the coral, they were as bright and new as if they had just been minted, and local experts were able to tell us at once that they were Mogul rupees, made in Surat (northwest India) in the year 1702.

We knew nothing about Indian history, but we started learning fast. The coins had been minted in the reign of the Emperor Aurangzeb, who was the last of the great Mogul rulers of India. (His mother lies in the most famous tomb in the world, the Taj Mahal.) He was master of India for almost half a century, from 1658 to 1707, but when he died, his empire broke up in civil wars which paved the way for the Western invaders—the Portuguese, the French, and finally the British.

One of the most interesting facts about these coins was that they all bore the same date. This strongly suggested that they were part of an official consignment, straight from the mint. And when I weighed the big lumps that Mike and the boys had brought back, I found that each contained almost exactly one thousand coins. There could be no doubt that they were the remains of 1,000-rupee bags that had been counted and then sealed—just as bags of coins are handled by banks today. When the ship had gone down, the material of the bags had lasted long enough for the outer layers of rupees to become cemented together by the action of the sea. Thus those inside the lump were perfectly preserved, while the whole mass retained the shape of the original bag.

When we read accounts of other treasure discoveries, we were interested to see how often this happens. Perhaps

Coins after cleaning. Note (right) Muslim date, 1113 (= 1702 A.D.).

the most successful treasure hunt of all times was that of
William Phips to the Silver Shoals, north of Haiti, where
a Spanish galleon carrying an enormous cargo of silver
went down in 1641. Captain Phips led a salvage fleet to
the area in 1687 and recovered coins and bullion to the
value of about $700,000 (several millions in today's
money). Here is an account, by an eyewitness, of the
treasure as it was hauled in:

. . . And so the dollars they hoisted in by whole chests of

44

2000 dollars together, for although the chests were rotted
off and consumed, yet the dollars, with rust, were so grown
together that they hung together as one lump—although
the middlemost of the chest was bright and sound—and
not many of them was much wasted by the water.

This was the state of the treasure only forty-six years
after it had sunk; ours was in exactly the same condition
260 years later. One of the lumps (now in the Smithsonian
Institution) still carried pieces of sacking from the original bags, stuck in cracks between the coins.

Altogether, Mike and the boys had brought back about
five thousand rupees, and we knew that government and
trading ships of this period often carried fifty times as
much. Judging by the guns and anchors, our wreck was a
fairly large vessel, so unless—by incredible luck—the expedition had just happened to hit on the captain's chest,
there must be lots more silver lying round somewhere.

I tried to get a picture of the situation by quizzing Mark
and Bobby, with rather tantalizing results—as shown by
this tape-recorded example:

CLARKE: What area would you say the coins covered. How
  big an area?
KRIEGEL: Well, the coins are in the bottom, next to the
  cannon—about five feet long and, say, up to two
  feet wide. Then if you went along a side of the

wall, I'd say it could have got down to six feet long and still about two, two and a half feet wide. But this wall was perpendicular to the bottom of the sand, so if it was laid over flat, it would probably be three feet wide.

CLARKE: You mean there were some coins in this wall?

KRIEGEL: On the surface of the wall we could see there were some coins and knocked three or four hunks off this wall; I mean by hunks about a thousand coins stuck together.

CLARKE: Well, those are quite sizeable lumps, because I've calculated that one of these thirty pound lumps does contain just about a thousand coins. And you mean to say that this wall was really made of lumps of coins?

KRIEGEL: Well, it seemed to be. As far as we could see, it was made of lumps of coins. . . .

A wall of solid silver! That was certainly an exciting prospect; there was no doubt that we would have to go back next year when the monsoon had passed and the reef was calm again. But could we keep such a secret for a whole year? It would be a terrible strain on us all.

Security was one worry; getting a boat for the job was another. It was obvious that we would need one big enough to carry two or three divers with all their equipment, and seaworthy enough to be safe if it was caught out on the reef in bad weather. Unfortunately we couldn't possibly afford such a boat.

I suggested trying to hire one, but Mike had more ambitious ideas. He would not be satisfied unless we had a boat all our own—one in which we could live and sleep and cook our meals, and be completely independent. Such a boat, I pointed out, would cost at least $10,000; where would we get the money?

Mike had the answer, and it shook me. He would make it in the local movie business. He planned to write, direct, and photograph an adventure film about sunken treasure—and it would be the first ever to be shot with *genuine* sunken treasure. What was more, it would be in Technicolor, and it would last two and a half hours—which is the length the audiences in the East demand for their main features.

Although at this point Mike had only made one 25-minute film on 16-millimeter Kodachrome—*Beneath the Seas of Ceylon*—he'd had some training in movie-making that many people would envy. Just a few years earlier he'd watched David Lean direct one of the great classics of modern cinema, *The Bridge on the River Kwai.* So he went ahead writing the script, assembling his unit, chasing bankers and film distributors, and doing all the thousand and one things that are necessary if one wants to make a movie.

The next six months were rather hectic for both of us. While Mike was planning his big production I flew from Ceylon to London to New York to Los Angeles and back again. For about this time Dr. Wernher von Braun, whom I'd converted to skin diving during a weekend in Washington several years ago, asked me to run a big panel discussion being arranged by the American Rocket Society in New York. Although I had to start thinking about space again, Mike's treasure ship was never far from my mind and I discussed it—cautiously—with all the experts I met. These included Mendel Peterson, world-famous authority on marine history at the Smithsonian Institution in Washington, and Luis Marden of the National Geographic Society, who not long ago had been diving on the remains of the *Bounty*.

And in Washington I was pleased to meet Mark Smith again, though I do not think that Mark was so pleased to be there. He obviously missed Ceylon. Both he and Bobby Kriegel had returned to the United States when their fathers' tours of duty in the East had finished. The boys will certainly never forget the Great Basses Reef, and I am afraid that all the skin diving they do in the future will be something of an anticlimax; for who can hope to find a treasure ship *twice* in one lifetime?

5. The Stars in Their Courses

When I got back to Ceylon, I was pleased (and surprised) to find how much progress had been made on the movie. And the boat was half built. Mike took me down to the shipyard to see the twenty-six-foot hull, very strongly made of timber about two inches thick. As yet it had no engines, but it did have a name—*Ran Muthu*.

This, I should explain, is Sinhalese for "pearls (and) gold"; it was a reference to the title of Mike's movie, *Ranmuthu Duwa*—"The Island of Pearls and Gold." By this time it was not clear if the movie was going to pay for the boat or the boat for the movie; nor is it clear to this day.

All the time bits and pieces for the expedition were arriving; it is absolutely incredible how much equipment one needs for an underwater treasure hunt. Perhaps the most essential item was the compressor for our Aqua-Lungs, which had to be pumped up with air to a pressure of over a ton on every square inch. This requires a very special kind of compressor (about twenty times as powerful as those used by garages for inflating tires) and it had to be portable so that we could use it in out-of-the-way places, or even on the boat. A very neat and compact unit, the Stewart-Warner Corporation's Cornelius 380 was flown out to us from the States. It could be easily carried by two men, yet would pump up an Aqua-Lung tank in only fifteen minutes.

Almost equally important were two rubber boats, very kindly given to us by the Avon Rubber Company of England. Although they folded up into a bag that could be stowed in the back of a car, these "Redshank" dinghies could carry half a dozen men and several hundred pounds of equipment. As you will soon appreciate, our job would have been absolutely impossible without them.

It was going to be impossible in any case, according to a large body of opinion. For long before we could get back to the reef, the world was coming to an end.

On February 5, 1962, there would be a total eclipse of the sun. That is a common enough phenomenon; it happens once or twice in every year. But this time something else would happen. All the planets visible to the naked eye—Mercury, Venus, Mars, Jupiter, and Saturn—would be in a compact group close to the sun; and the astrologers were sure that this heralded disaster.

As a matter of fact, such close planetary groupings happen about once every century (the next will be on May 5, 2000), and I wrote several articles for the local newspapers pointing this out. These helped to reassure some people, but not many. Even those who thought there was "nothing in it" felt it wise to take precautions; there were offerings and prayers all over Asia, and in the temples the monks were chanting night and day. Only a few national leaders, like Mr. Nehru, had the courage to stand up and say that these predictions were all nonsense.

February 5 dawned and went; absolutely nothing happened, except that some indignant clients assaulted the astrologers and demanded their money back. We continued to shoot the film and to get the boat ready for the expedition, now planned for next month.

Fatal February drew to a close; it had not brought the end of the world. But then, on its very last day, it nearly brought the end of me.

I was shopping in Colombo, buying equipment for the boat; most of our time now seemed to be spent buying equipment for the boat. Leaving one store, I misjudged the height of a doorway and crashed the top of my head against the lintel. It took me a few minutes to recover, and I had a painful scalp wound; but I felt none the worse. I got on my motor scooter, drove three miles home, played several vigorous games of table tennis, and ate a hearty dinner— my last for several months.

That night I became violently sick and spent the next couple of days in bed. But convinced that it was merely something I'd eaten (you get used to occasional stomach upsets in the East), I was not particularly worried, and never dreamed of calling in the doctor. By the time one did arrive on the scene, I had become almost completely paralyzed and could barely breathe. Perhaps luckily, I was also delirious, so I had no idea how ill I was.

After six weeks of being fed and bathed like a baby, in a private hospital, I was carried home at just about the time we had planned to leave for the reef. The Great Basses wreck would be undisturbed for 1962, and it seemed most unlikely that it would ever be disturbed by me at *any* future date. Though I could sit up when propped in a chair, I was stuck there and had to ring a bell for help when I wanted to move. The doctors, who had diagnosed an unusual form of spinal injury, promised that I would be able to walk again, though they warned me that my left arm would never be much good (it now looked as if it were constructed of matchsticks). Any more underwater activity was almost certainly out of the question.

I was not too unhappy; I could read and write and was in no pain. After a while, when hoisted to my feet, I was able to wobble a few dozen yards with the aid of sticks. Meanwhile Mike, having canceled the expedition and knowing that I was left in good hands, had flown to England to finish the editing and sound track of *Ranmuthu Duwa*.

Presently I felt the creative urge again and began working on the boys' book about the sea, called *Dolphin Island*. I wrote a couple of pages every day in pencil while I was propped up in my chair and got my secretary to type them out while I could still remember what the squiggles meant. *Dolphin Island* went very smoothly, but I felt rather sad when it was finished. I could not help thinking that it was probably my farewell to the sea, which had given me so many strange, wonderful, and exciting experiences.

Then all else was banished by the arrival of Mike's

53

movie, which we had been awaiting for weeks with growing impatience and anxiety. We rushed the seventeen large cans of film around to a local cinema, and two and a half hours later emerged feeling on top of the world. There was no doubt that Mike and his little team of co-workers had made a winner. There were a few rough patches, but on the whole *Ranmuthu Duwa* was completely professional, and the color was lovely. RMD (as we now called it) was, in fact, the first Sinhalese color film ever made, and I have never grown tired of watching the scenes of dawn over the great temples, the sea-washed cliffs of Trincomalee, the lines of pilgrims descending the sacred mountain known as Adam's Peak, and the mysterious underwater sequences—many of them shot on the Great Basses. For a first attempt at professional movie-making it was an astonishing accomplishment.

RMD turned out to be a smash hit, and its catchy theme tunes were soon blaring out of every radio. Within a few months it had been seen by a million people—a tenth of the population of the country—and had created a great reservoir of good will for us. Wherever we went the members of our team who had played parts in the movie were recognized and cheered (if they were Good Guys) or hissed (if they weren't).

With the film finished and running in twelve movie houses all around Ceylon, Mike could now concentrate

54

on the boat. At last, one bright Sunday in October, it was finished, and its twin diesels took us on a grand tour round the port of Colombo, which is one of the biggest artificial harbors in the world. We anchored for tea in the shadows of great ocean liners weighing ten thousand times as much as little *Ran Muthu* and watched with fascination as our echo sounder traced the contours of the sea bed.

Everything was working fine; everything, that is, except me.

6. False Starts and Alarms

Even three months before the 1963 expedition was due to start, I was not sure if I could go with it. I could now walk steadily, though slowly, and was swimming every day, even more slowly. I had also made a couple of Aqua-Lung dives in the local pool and found that I could breathe quite comfortably underwater. This was encouraging; ten months earlier I had been barely able to breathe on land.

So while Mike worked on *Ran Muthu* I exercised and trained and weightlifted (very small weights). By the time the boat was ready to sail I hoped that I would be able to watch operations without getting in the way, even if I could not do any diving myself.

Ran Muthu left Colombo on March 16, 1963, and she only just made it. The sixteenth was a Saturday, and the lock gates through which she had to pass shut at noon for the weekend. We spent the entire morning, starting at 5 A.M., in one frantic rush, trying to get hold of essential items which had been forgotten until the last moment. But when I arrived at the shipyard at 10 A.M., I was astonished to see how neatly Mike had stowed away a small mountain of equipment aboard the boat, tucking it into her numerous lockers and cupboards.

She had about fifteen minutes to spare when she chugged away across the little lake, in the very center of the city, on which she had been built. (If you imagine the Central Park lake or the Serpentine with a shipyard on it, you have a rough idea of the situation in Colombo.) To get from the lake to the harbor the boat had to pass first through a lock where the water level dropped about ten feet, and then through a large tunnel which actually ran under some of the main roads of the city. So part of *Ran Muthu*'s journey out to sea was by subway.

Ran Muthu *loading, Colombo.*

The beginning of the adventure. Dwarfed by the surrounding ships, Ran Muthu *leaves Colombo Harbor.*

By jumping on my motor scooter (the doctors did not approve, but it was great for my morale to be able to move around on my own), I was able to catch the boat at strategic points and take photos of the voyagers as they left on their adventure. *Ran Muthu* looked incredibly tiny as she sailed through the harbor past the ocean liners and freighters that visit Colombo from almost every port in the world. I caught my last glimpse of her as she was passing the lighthouse at the end of the enormous sea wall that guards the harbor from the monsoon gales. Mike had a tape recorder on board, with several spools of music, and as *Ran Muthu* headed south down the coast I could

hear faintly, drifting across the Indian Ocean, "The Ride of the Valkyrie." Then I went home and started my own packing.

Late the next day Mike phoned from the south coast village of Tangalle with the news that they had managed to creep into harbor on half an engine, and that the weather was not good. I arranged for a mechanic and spare parts to be rushed down to him, and set off myself the next day in a beat-up Austin van, loaded with cameras, air compressor, and the delicate equipment we did not wish to send by sea. I hoped that by the time I arrived, the engines would be working and the weather improved.

In any case, Tangalle, with a magnificent sweep of bay, is such a beautiful spot that I'd be quite content to stay there indefinitely. We checked into the resthouse—Ceylon's nearest equivalent to a motel, though I had better warn prospective visitors right away that many of them are more picturesque than sanitary. Driven out of the best room by bugs, we retreated in good order behind a barrage of DDT. But we were well fed and so were prepared to put up with a few minor inconveniences. That was just as well, because we were to be stuck here, less than fifty miles from our objective, for almost a month.

I won't bother to list all the frustrations and minor disasters that kept us trapped at Tangalle. What it really added up to was that when the engines were O.K., the

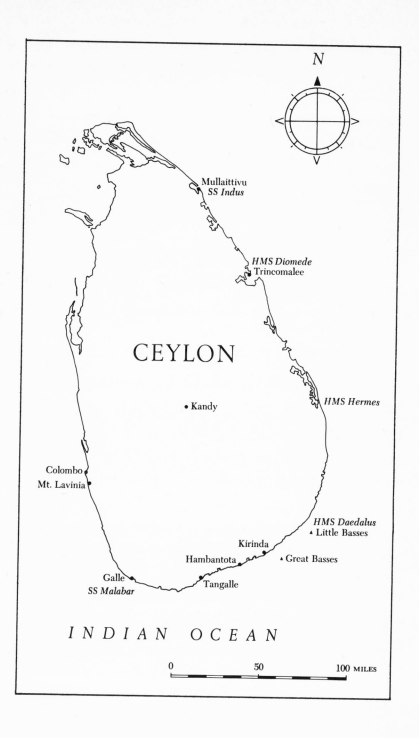

N

Mullaittivu
SS *Indus*

HMS Diomede
Trincomalee

CEYLON

• Kandy

HMS Hermes

Colombo
Mt. Lavinia

HMS Daedalus
▲ Little Basses

Kirinda
Hambantota   ▲ Great Basses

Galle
SS *Malabar*   Tangalle

INDIAN   OCEAN

0   50   100 MILES

Tangalle resthouse. Martin, a member of the crew, brings ashore the broken exhaust.

weather wasn't—and vice versa. And in the middle of all this, Mike's wife Elizabeth presented him with their first child, a baby daughter.

The arrival of the baby caused a major crisis in our plans. For though she was a fine little girl, it was necessary to give her a complete blood transfusion and to keep her under observation for some time. Until he was sure that she was quite safe, Mike couldn't possibly leave home, so the expedition had to mark time back in Colombo. And it was at this very moment that we received news that our rivals—the divers who had killed our tame groupers—were on their way back to the reef.

We had done our best, of course, to disguise our objective, but it is hard to keep a secret in Ceylon, and by this time anyone who was interested must have had a very good idea just why *Ran Muthu* was hanging around the south coast. We could hardly blame poor little baby Anne for keeping us biting our fingernails in Colombo, but I could see a fortune slipping from our grasp while we waited for the doctors to give the all-clear.

As you can guess, it was a rather nerve-wracking time. However, our delay in Colombo brought us one piece of good luck. On the auspicious day of April 1 we received a letter from a certain Peter Throckmorton in Athens, saying that he'd been working on numerous wrecks of archaeological importance in the Mediterranean and Aegean, and would we let him know if there was anything interesting around Ceylon?

The writer's name was familiar, and when I ran through my files of the *National Geographic* I quickly discovered why. Peter Throckmorton had been responsible for the discovery and excavation, with a team from the University of Pennsylvania, of the oldest wreck ever found—a 1300 B.C. Bronze Age trader that had gone down on a reef off the coast of Turkey.

His accounts of this fascinating and most important

discovery have been published in the *National Geographic* for May, 1962 ("Oldest Known Shipwreck Yields Bronze-Age Cargo") and May, 1960 ("Thirty-three Centuries Under the Sea"). When we read these articles and studied the techniques used to investigate this incredibly ancient wreck, we knew at once that we needed Peter Throckmorton's experience very badly on our own expedition. But we hoped to leave again in two or three days, and we were not even sure if he was still in Athens, still less what his timetable was.

We took a chance and cabled: "Can you come if we send return air ticket? Can promise interesting wreck." I might add that at the time we didn't have the money for the ticket, but I happen to own an Air Travel Credit Card, which enables you to buy now and face the consequences later.

While we waited to hear from Peter Throckmorton and Mike was hovering round the nursing home keeping an eye on the baby's progress, I decided to take another quick run down the coast to check on conditions there—by which I mean the weather and our potential rivals.

At Tangalle *Ran Muthu* was still riding patiently at anchor, looked after by the skeleton crew we had left aboard. Rodney Jonklaas, who had been busy in the area hunting the tropical fish which he exports all over the world, said that conditions had been good and that there

Ran Muthu *loading, Tangalle. Martin rows dinghy to boat.*

was no sign of any other expedition. It was true that some suspicious characters had been making inquiries about our activities, but there was good reason to think that we need no longer worry about the competition. On the way down the coast we had passed the only other diving boat in the island, and it looked in such a decrepit condition that we felt safe in writing it off.

Though the weather was fine at Tangalle and the little bay looked as beautiful as ever with its fishing boats bobbing in the sun, this did not mean that conditions were good fifty miles away at the Great Basses Reef, off a much more exposed and open coast. So a companion and I drove on to Kirinda, which I had not seen since I accompanied Mike and Rodney to the lighthouse four years before.

The sea was fairly calm, with small breakers making halfhearted assaults on the beach from time to time. But what was it like out at the lighthouse, just visible ten miles away as a tiny mark on the horizon? There was one way to find out.

I had brought with me, for this very purpose, the finest small telescope that has ever been built—the 3½-inch Questar. Because it uses both mirrors *and* lenses, so that the light rays are reflected several times along the tube, it is incredibly compact and weighs less than ten pounds. Yet it is a complete astronomical observatory, with a built-in clock drive that will keep it following the same star all night. It has been used to take quite astonishing close-ups of the moon, at magnifications of over two hundred. (If this sounds like an advertisement for the Questar, that's fine. But I'd better warn prospective buyers that it costs $995.)

A small hill, or rather a giant rock, looms above the village of Kirinda, and from its summit one can get a marvelous view of the surrounding landscape. On the top of the hill is an attractive little Buddhist shrine, and

66

we climbed up to this carrying Questar and tripod. After paying our respects to the *bikkhu* (monk), we set up the telescope and I gazed out to sea.

There was the lighthouse, poised on the very rim of the world. In this tropical heat, with the sun burning down from overhead, the atmosphere danced and trembled, and the image was never still for an instant. But as I stared through the eyepiece and waited for the fleeting moments when the picture steadied itself, I could pick out a whole host of familiar details on that rock ten miles away in the Indian Ocean.

I could see the crane that had hauled us and our gear from the relief boat four years ago. There were men moving around on the lower platform; had the atmosphere been steady enough for me to use the full power of the telescope, I might have been able to recognize them. The weathervane and the great lamphouse were easily visible; I could even catch occasional glimpses of the massive diamond-shaped panes of glass which protected the light. Oddest of all, from my viewpoint, two of the tower's deeply recessed windows were exactly in line, so I could look straight through the middle of the lighthouse into a patch of blue sky.

But the reef was what really interested me. I scanned the telescope along the horizon—and there it was. Unmistakable on the skyline was the dark triangle I had

Air view of Kirinda, showing the shrine from which the reef operations were observed and photographed. The Great Basses Reef is on the horizon but invisible. ROYAL CEYLON AIR FORCE

The Great Basses Reef. Shark's Tooth Rock in center.

christened Shark's Tooth Rock. The highest part of the reef, it must have claimed many ships over the centuries; to us it was useful as a landmark. By taking a sight on it, Mike would locate the wreck with complete accuracy, in the classic pirate-treasure tradition.

Around Shark's Tooth Rock the sea was never still. But it was breaking lazily, without violence. Most of the time the rock was completely exposed; only once in every few minutes did the swell surge over it or a curtain of spray hide it momentarily from view. As far as I could judge, it would be safe to dive there.

Like Moses looking into the Promised Land, I stared

70

at that remote and tantalizing patch of sea foaming whitely on the horizon. After all the difficulties and disappointments we had already endured, would we *ever* get there? And would it be worth the trouble—or had Mike and the boys found everything that mattered?

In a few days we would know the answers.

7. Kirinda Beach

When I got back to Colombo to report that all was well, Mike had good news for me. Peter Throckmorton had cabled to say that he could come, so I dusted the cobwebs off my Air Travel Card and booked his ticket. He arrived four days later, loaded with specialized underwater equipment, such as a pair of Captain Cousteau's neat little Calypso cameras, which work above or below water with equal ease, and a submarine balloon for hoisting heavy objects from the sea bed. He also brought with him a fascinating collection of color slides of his 3,200-year-old Bronze Age cargo ship and gave us an illustrated lecture that very night. We had been afraid that he would look down on our little wreck, since his was more than ten times older, but he was quite excited by the samples we showed him—the first genuine treasure he had ever seen.

We left the next afternoon on what we hoped would be our final attempt to reach the reef. I was getting seriously alarmed about all these delays. What if the southwest monsoon was early this year, as was sometimes the case? Then there would be no hope of doing any diving, and the boat might be trapped on the open, exposed south coast of the island, where good harbors were few and far between.

By the end of the five-hour drive to Tangalle we had grown to know a lot about Peter and were very happy to have him with us. Apart from being one of the world's very few experts on underwater archaeology (though he would deny this), he was excellent company and possessed an unusual collection of talents. These will emerge later in this book (we were still discovering them when he left), but we were already awed to find that he was either fluent or could make himself understood in Japanese, Hawaiian, Tahitian, Turkish, Greek, French, and German. Before he left the island, he was making progress with Sinhalese and had picked up more words than I had in five years.

Ran Muthu and crew were still waiting patiently at Tangalle, but the weather did not look at all promising. It was dull and windy, and the sea was quite choppy; nevertheless, Mike determined to set sail. Even if he could not reach Kirinda, he would put into the next port of call —the small town of Hambantota, roughly at the halfway mark.

As I watched *Ran Muthu* bucking her way out to sea I was heartily glad that I was not aboard her, and was not at all surprised when she turned back after only fifteen minutes. But the mariners had not been beaten by the weather; one of the engine exhausts had broken and was belching diesel smoke into the boat. There was nothing to do but to wait at Tangalle, fuming almost as badly as the engine, until we could get a replacement rushed down from Colombo.

By noon the next day the repair had been made (so we thought) and *Ran Muthu* got out to sea again, with Mike, Peter, and the two boatmen aboard. We of the shore party waited until they were safely out of sight, in case of any more false alarms; then we packed all the rest of the gear and drove along the coast to Hambantota, where the boat should arrive in the late afternoon.

We stopped once at a headland on the way and looked out to sea through the telescope—and there she was, coming along nicely. But when she caught up with us at the harbor, there was bad news. This morning's "repaired" exhaust had broken again.

So we spent the evening in Hambantota while the repair was repaired; this time such a thorough welding job was done that we were quite sure it would hold. The next morning, confident that *Ran Muthu* would catch up with us, we drove the final lap to Kirinda, intending to unpack our equipment and establish our shore base so

Our hotel. Inside the boat shed, Kirinda.

that everything would be ready when the boat arrived.

At this point I think it will be a good idea to list the complete cast of our mammoth production so that you know who was who and what they did. Here it is:

ABOARD THE BOAT

Peter Throckmorton   (*diver, photographer, archaeologist*)

Mike Wilson   (*diver, film director*)

Martin
Laza   } (*boatmen, mechanics*)

WITH THE LAND PARTY

Hector Ekanayake   (*boxer, diver photographer, film actor*)

A. P. Peiris   (*still and movie photographer*)

Myself

Rodney Jonklaas (diver, marine zoologist) arrived under his own power in his Volkswagen and brought with him perhaps the most important man of the expedition—the cook, Anthony.

Our living arrangements were simple and rugged. We just moved into the Imperial Lighthouse Service's shed, which we shared with the launch *Pharos II* and the staff on shore duty. We had brought some camp beds, but not enough, and the lighthouse staff kindly loaned us spare blankets and cots, and moved into odd corners of the shed to make room for us. When we had unloaded all our Aqua-Lung cylinders, cameras, stores, diving gear, and personal kits, there was very little floor space left.

We were fairly well organized by the middle of the morning when *Ran Muthu* came around the rocky headland beneath the shrine and anchored out in the bay, some two hundred yards from shore. It was not safe to bring her in any closer, for if she dragged anchor in the night, she could easily go aground on the gently shelving beach; but the invaluable rubber dinghies allowed us to shuttle back and forth without any trouble.

As soon as the crew came ashore, they brought depressing news. Yes, the exhaust had broken yet again. Not in the place mended twice during the last thirty-six hours, but practically everywhere else. The whole system of flexible pipes was coming apart; however, the versatile Peter thought he could fix it, and he worked all afternoon with Martin and Laza in the hot, pitching boat. By nightfall they had completed the job, as far as it could be done, and came ashore for dinner.

Our patient cook, Anthony, working on the beach with two or three pots and pans and a smoking wood fire that I found impossible to approach without suffocation, produced a fine meal of fried fish and *iced* fruit salad. For this last miracle we could again thank Rodney, who has spent so much time in jungles and other god-forsaken places

77

that he has developed a great talent for making himself comfortable. He had brought with him a huge icebox, and we used this to store our perishable food and cold drinks.

I have seldom slept more soundly than on that rough canvas cot, tucked under the side of the lighthouse relief launch in that shed on Kirinda Beach. Once a passing shower woke me, for I had been unfortunate enough to place my bed immediately under a hole in the roof, but even this seemed only an amusing trifle. Being careful not to disturb the other sleepers, I moved the cot a few inches and, as the rain had stopped almost as soon as it had started, tiptoed out to look at the weather.

It was wonderfully peaceful on the great empty arc of sand curving away for miles beneath the waning moon. The outrigger fishing boats drawn up on the beach, waiting to depart before dawn, looked strange and mysterious in the pale moonlight. The sea was very calm, and only a few little waves came rippling up to my feet.

Suddenly, far out at sea, a ruby star pulsed once on the horizon. The rotating beams from the Great Basses lighthouse, ten miles away, were sweeping patiently around the sky, as they had done every night for ninety years. I was not the only person awake here in the small hours before the equatorial dawn; out there one of the lightkeepers was on duty, tending the great lantern in its granite tower a hundred feet above the rocks.

Kirinda Beach.

Yes, it was peaceful and lovely now; but what would it be like on this exposed and open bay on a pitch-black, moonless night, when the monsoon gales were howling and the great waves came thundering up the beach? And that time was approaching fast; we would need better luck than we had had so far if we were to explore that tantalizing wreck. For if we left it too late, the Great Basses would claim one more victim.

8. *Through the Reef*

Four hundred miles from the equator the days and nights are practically the same length the whole year round. The sun always rises at 6 A.M. and sets at 6 P.M., to within a few minutes; there are none of the long summer days or winter nights that we know in northern latitudes. This gives life a certain monotony, geared as it is to twelve hours of darkness and twelve hours of light.

We quickly adapted ourselves to this routine and were already moving around in the brief morning twilight before the dawn broke. After a hasty breakfast we checked the gear and loaded it into the rubber boats. Before 9 A.M. *Ran Muthu* was on her way to the reef.

Though Mike had pressed me to come, I was not aboard. The boat was already crowded, and on this first day I decided to stay on land. I was still extremely weak, and if anything went wrong, I would only be in the way. Moreover, I wanted a full report on conditions at the reef before I would risk going out, even as a sightseer.

There was plenty to do on land. Our activities around the boathouse had attracted a great deal of local interest; we were probably the most exciting thing that had happened at Kirinda for years. Crowds of curious onlookers watched our every move, and I realized that this might be embarrassing if we did find anything valuable in the wreck. It was hard enough to keep an eye on our equipment, especially as hordes of small children were always hovering around and would not be shooed away. Several items disappeared during our visit, including an Aqua-Lung pressure gauge of Rodney's, of no use to anyone else, but invaluable to him. On the whole, however, we did not do badly; if the locals had been so inclined, they

81

could have skinned us clean.

Celyon is a mixture of many races, the two main groups being the Sinhalese (mostly Buddhist) and the Tamils (mostly Hindu). Together these make up over ninety per cent of the total population. The inhabitants of Kirinda, however, belong to a small minority group; they are Muslims, and many of them show clear signs of their Malay origin. During the nineteenth century a regiment of Malay troops had been disbanded here and had settled down as farmers and fishermen. Their descendants still speak Malay, though they all understand Sinhalese and Tamil and often English as well.

We often wondered what they thought about our activities; though the youngsters were friendly, it was impossible to establish contact with the adults. They stood around watching us, usually without any signs of emotion; but one day a wispy, bleary-eyed elder, whom we christened the Mad Mullah, stationed himself outside the shed and delivered an impassioned address to anyone who would listen. Whether he was calling upon the faithful to unite against the infidels who were looting the treasures that rightly belonged to them, we never knew.

On that first morning I waited until *Ran Muthu* had had time to get out of the reef and then carried the Questar up to the top of the little hill. There again was the lighthouse, gleaming whitely in the sun; there was Shark's Tooth

Rock, with the breakers foaming around it. And there, rising and falling above the surf, was *Ran Muthu*'s canvas awning, which gave her the appearance of a sea-going jeep.

She was stationed on the landward side of the reef, and through the telescope it was quite hair-raising to see how she appeared to be completely submerged in the boiling surf every time she sank in the trough of a wave. But I knew that this was an illusion; she was actually several hundred yards from the surf, anchored in smooth water. For the first time I realized the difficulties the divers would be facing; they would have to work right into that line of foam, in the danger area that *Ran Muthu* herself could never approach.

I watched for over an hour from the hilltop, wondering what was happening out there on the horizon. From time to time, far out in the Indian Ocean, an oil tanker or a freighter would go majestically past; this was a very busy spot, and I counted four large ships in half an hour. Usually their hulls were below the horizon, so I had a dramatic proof of the fact that the world is round. For I could see only the bridge at the center of a ship and the superstructure at its stern moving in splendid isolation along the skyline. At first glance it seemed as if two separate ships were sailing past—not one, half hidden by the curve of the globe.

At last, late in the afternoon, I saw that *Ran Muthu*

was moving away from her anchorage. She made a wide circuit around the boiling water of the reef, then passed in front of the lighthouse as she headed for home.

You can imagine with what eagerness I waited on the shore when *Ran Muthu* came around the headland and dropped anchor in the bay. I also counted the number of heads on board and was relieved to find that as many

Brandy and soda-water bottles, intact and cemented together by coral, from mid-nineteenth century wreck.

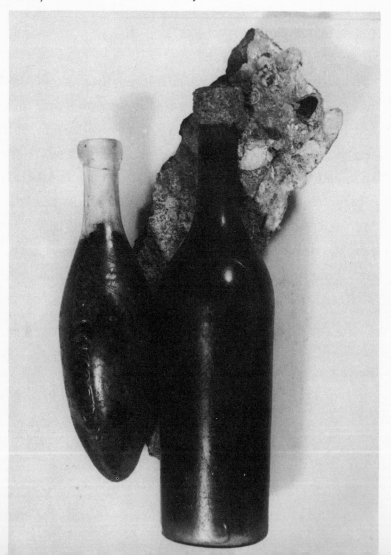

were coming back as had gone out. A few minutes later the rubber dinghy, chugging along with its little outboard motor, brought the divers back to land.

Peter stepped ashore, staggering under the weight of a heavy sack, which seemed likely to arouse all sorts of local suspicions. By this time, of course, there was such an enormous crowd that we had to push our way through it to carry the equipment back to the shed—though some of the friendlier young Kirindans helped us with the Aqua-Lung cylinders.

We did our best to divert attention from the sack by showing some of the other finds, which were quite surprising. Of all things, Mike and Peter had brought back a large number of empty soda-water bottles from the reef.

They weren't like any soda-water bottles I'd ever seen before; they had pointed bases, like the ancient amphorae, or wine jars, that litter the bottom of the Mediterranean, so they could lie only on their sides. But the biggest surprise, from my point of view, was the raised lettering on the green-tinted glass:

CLARKE-ROMER & CO.

CEYLON

SUPERIOR SODA WATER

It gave me an odd feeling to see my own name emerging from the sea in this relic of a forgotten marine tragedy.

I knew at once, of course, that it had nothing to do with the silver wreck; I felt certain that no one had been bottling soda water around 1702. (Though I was very much surprised to discover that they had started to do so by the end of that same century!) When we had all settled down in the boat shed, Mike and Peter told me what had happened.

Though the sea was very calm when they arrived at the reef, there was a big swell breaking over the exposed rocks. They had anchored *Ran Muthu* on the landward side of the reef, in the more sheltered water. When the divers had put on their Aqua-Lungs and gone down, *there* was a splendid wreck almost immediately beneath them.

It was quite a large ship—about 150 feet long—and had obviously hit the reef from the seaward side and then been carried right over it, to settle down in shallow, fairly sheltered water. It was completely broken up and seemed to be a century old, though this could be no more than an educated guess. Besides a mass of ballast stones, the wreck was littered with many badly corroded iron spheres, which looked as if they might be mortar shells. Mike also found some lead plugs, marked with the broad arrow— the official sign of the British Government.

But the soda-water bottles were the really intriguing items, and we hoped that they would give us a clue to the

Through the reef.

date of the wreck. Underwater archaeology is like a detective story, and the most trivial items can sometimes lead to important discoveries. Mixed with the soda-water bottles there were also many brandy bottles, and Mike and Peter actually retrieved a brandy-and-soda—the two bottles cemented together by coral, unbroken after at least a hundred years on this storm-lashed reef. I could not help wondering about all this brandy: had it helped to cause the wreck?

Interesting though it was, this relatively modern wreck was only a diversion from the main objective, and the divers devoted little time to it. Then Mike led them off on the long, hard swim through the reef to the site that he had last visited with Bobby and Mark two years before.

Mike has a wonderful sense of direction, and he needed it in this complicated and dangerous territory of rocks and gulleys, with the surf breaking on all sides. As they got further into the reef they had to go deep to avoid the foam; there is nothing more terrifying than swimming blind, in seething white water, expecting your face mask to smash against a rock at any moment. At this point there was a convenient cave through the reef which allowed them to take a short-cut—and here Rodney's diving career nearly came to an end.

For some time a small amount of water had been coming through his mouthpiece, but he had ignored it as it did not seem dangerous. But when he reached the floor of the cave, he found that he was getting no air at all; the mouthpiece was feeding him nothing but seawater. He was barely able to turn back through the cave, swim out under the line of foam, and reach the surface. Rodney himself considers this one of his narrowest underwater escapes. I very much doubt that many divers could have made it.

He went straight back to the boat, switched to a new regulator, and then went after Mike and Peter again, but was unable to find his way through the gap that only Mike knew. After he had lost his way in a labyrinth of caves, he turned back; so he did not see the wreck that day.

But Mike led Peter straight to the site without a moment's hesitation, and I'll give Peter's own description of what they found—exactly as he dictated it that night into the tape recorder down on the deserted beach, with the murmur of the waves providing a soft background noise, and the ruby star of the lighthouse flashing on the horizon every forty-five seconds.

We anchored the boat to the north of the site, that is, the opposite side from where the swells were breaking, and we swam from the boat to the wreck site, which was probably a mistake because we had to swim against the current

Anchor from mid-nineteenth-century wreck.   RODNEY JONKLAAS, B.SC.

and we used up too much air getting there. Anyway, we got to the site. It was quite surprising for me because there were more fish on the reef than I'd ever seen anywhere in one place, except perhaps in places like Johnson Island and Christmas Island in the Central Pacific. Anyway, we swam through this—the surf breaking over the ridge of rock—and we swam through cracks, through ways in the rock that Mike knew, into the place where the coin wreck was. . . .

It seems very clear what happened to the wreck. The whole site is about sixty feet long. At one end there are two large iron anchors, that is, at the east end. Then, about twenty feet to the west—this channel in which the wreck lies runs almost due east and west—is a series of cannons jumbled together like matchsticks. I noticed about ten, although I didn't count them. . . . About twenty feet to the west of the cannons is a smaller brass cannon, about four feet long, in very good condition, almost completely covered with coral. . . . Where the brass cannon lies, the bottom is a mass of concreted corrosion products of iron, bits of silver coins, musket balls, and so forth. . . .

It seems obvious that the ship sank head down—went over the outer reef, bilged herself hopelessly, and sank right there. She probably went down bow first with her stern up, and hung on the reef, and I should think that with the cannons shaking up and down, the whole wreck pounding up and down, and big swells as there must have been when she went on the rocks, the cannons would have broken loose and slid down the deck to the

90

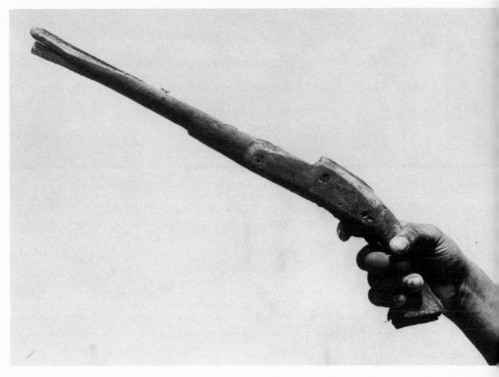

Wooden pistol stock. Almost all the iron has disappeared, but the wood is still sound. The thimble has been removed from the butt.

position where they are now. . . . Everything washed back and forth and stuck in crevices of the rock and jammed there together. . . .

Out of the wreck, during their first dive, Mike and Peter were able to chip all sorts of interesting items: the wooden stock of a pistol, musket balls, the rim of a silver bowl, and several cannon balls. These were actually shells—hollow spheres with traces of gunpowder still inside them.

All this material, mixed up with coral and stones from the sea bed, had been in the sack that Peter had humped ashore; it was not, as I had hoped, a solid mass of silver. But here and there, easy to miss unless you were looking for them, were the little disks of corroded coins. One or two were in good condition; and there was no mistaking them, with their curving Arabic inscriptions.

It was the right wreck. After two years Mike still knew his way through the labyrinth of the reef.

9. *The Mother Lode*

That first evening back from the reef set the pattern of all those to follow. We would unload and check the cameras, start pumping up the empty Aqua-Lung cylinders, see that *Ran Muthu* was securely anchored and with a light showing, and do all the dozens of other odd jobs

TOP: *Fragment of money chest, showing coin and piece of bag.*
MIDDLE: *Bronze thimbles from butts of paired pistols (note floral designs).* BOTTOM: *Bronze pestle (scale in centimeters).*

which are necessary to keep an underwater expedition functioning. The center of interest, however, was Peter.

He would sit at a bench, covered with the dirty smelly masses of rock that he and Mike had salvaged from the bottom of the sea, and chip patiently away at them for hour after hour. From time to time something of interest would emerge from the coral, and he would drop it into one of the many little tins and boxes he had set up.

To most people the objects he was collecting would hardly have seemed of much value or importance; to the archaeologist they were vital, for any one of them might provide the essential clue which would allow us to identify the wreck. Perhaps the most interesting and romantic item was a complete pitstol stock, the wood in quite good condition, but the metal of the barrel almost completely rusted away. It was one of a pair (the second was badly broken up) and the bronze plate, or thimble, covering the butt was in perfect condition, inscribed with a handsome floral design.

Peter also collected small fragments of wood from the broken-up hull of the ship and sealed them in plastic bags to prevent them from falling to pieces when they dried out. He hoped that experts might be able to identify not only the type of wood but even the part of the world where it had grown. In this way we might be able to discover where the ship was built.

From time to time, as Peter chipped his patient way through the lumps of coral, one of the Mogul rupees would come to light. Since all of Peter's operations were watched by a large crowd of spectators, we thought that the best thing to do was to show these frankly and to explain what they were, but to make no particular fuss about them. If we did try to hide them, that in itself would look suspicious; for, after all, one would expect to find *some* coins in an old wreck. We hoped that it would be obvious to our audience that we weren't going to make any fortunes this way, chipping out one or two rupees an hour.

Yet strangely enough, while we were engaged on this work, the shadow of the most famous treasure hunt of modern times fell across our little group. The lighthouse superintendent, Frank Rees, came to see how we were getting on, and he told us of his adventures on the evening of May 20, 1922.

He was aboard the eight-thousand-ton liner *Egypt* steaming through thick fog off the French coast on her way from London to Bombay. Suddenly out of the mist came the bows of a cargo steamer; the *Egypt* was struck amidships and sank in twenty minutes. Ninety-six people went down with her—plus seven tons of gold and silver.

Frank Rees was lucky. He walked off the deck straight into the water as the ship sank and was picked up two hours later, covered with oil and black soot. When he arrived at Brest, it took him some time to convince the French that he was not one of Egypt's native crew; and all this happened to him, memorably enough, on his twenty-first birthday.

The *Egypt* and her gold lay in four hundred feet of water—beyond the reach of ordinary divers even today. However, an Italian team developed observation chambers and grabs to work at this depth, and they blasted their way into the heart of the ship, cutting through deck after deck until they reached the strongroom. Weather conditions were so bad that work was possible for only a few weeks each year, and while they were engaged on another salvage job, the divers accidentally touched off thousands of tons of explosives in a sunken munitions ship. They were blown sky-high. But their successors continued the work on the *Egypt*, and in 1931, nearly ten

Rodney (left) and Peter examine the finds in the Kirinda boat shed.

years after it had gone down, three-quarters of the *Egypt's* gold was brought back to the light of day.

It was a good reminder to us of the tenacity with which the sea guards its treasures—not that we really needed one.

The next morning the sea was very calm and the sun was shining brilliantly in a clear sky. I would never have a better opportunity of watching the divers at work, so this time I was aboard *Ran Muthu* when she sailed.

The outrigger fishing boats, the shed that we had made our temporary home, the whitely gleaming shrine on its hilltop overlooking Kirinda—all fell slowly astern as we chugged out to sea. After an hour's run the coast of Ceylon seemed very far away, and the tower of the lighthouse was looming up ahead, dominating the horizon.

It was about here that I lost my breakfast. I am normally quite a good sailor, but I'd found a sure-fire recipe for seasickness. It is to concentrate on taking photographs through the finder of a miniature camera, aboard a slowly pitching boat. Waiting for the horizon to come horizontal is a good test for any stomach.

When we got to the reef, Mike took the boat cautiously around it and anchored this time on the seaward side, about a hundred yards from the breakers. He did not propose to swim through those coral caves again.

Rodney, Mike, and Peter put on their Aqua-Lungs and

dropped overboard. I remember my gasp of astonishment when they submerged, and I saw how startlingly brilliant the colors on their clothes and equipment remained as they sank down into the water. I had quite forgotten how pure and transparent this ocean water could be, and its crystal depths looked very attractive. I no longer had any hesitation about going in, though I did not feel strong enough to handle an Aqua-Lung; I much preferred to make my first dive unencumbered.

Putting on flippers, face mask, gloves, and weight belt, I gripped the snorkel tube between my teeth and lowered myself into the water. I was taking no chances at all, but hung on to the side of the rubber dinghy while Laza rowed it over to the reef to join the other divers.

The view beneath me, though wonderfully clear, was not very impressive. I was snorkling across a rocky sea bed with no coral, little marine growth, and very few fish. But as I approached the reef the underwater terrain became much more rugged, dropping away into numerous pits and gulleys.

I also began to feel the first ominous tug of the swell that was surging over the reef, even on this calm day. Laza brought the rubber dinghy to rest about fifty feet away from the line of foam, and some two hundred feet from *Ran Muthu*. He would keep station here so that if the divers got into trouble, they would find help at once as

Dinghy on station above divers. Laza watches out for breakers.

soon as they surfaced. However, it was not safe even for the dinghy to remain too near the wreck site; Laza had to keep his distance and watch out for any sudden waves that might surge up and sweep him onto the reef.

As soon as the dinghy came to a halt, I could see the divers at work, though they were still fifty feet away and thirty feet down. Hanging on to a rope from the dinghy —I was being ultra-cautious, and with good reason—I swam over to them and had a perfect bird's-eye view of operations.

100

General view of wreck site. Peter is working over bronze cannon.
RODNEY JONKLAAS, B.SC.

The first thing I noticed was a small cannon, half buried in the coral that had grown around it during two and a half centuries. (Coral can do far better than that, but on this exposed and wave-swept site it had made very slow progress—luckily for us.) There was nothing else that would have caught my eye had I been swimming casually across this section of the reef.

Rodney's fine "aerial" photograph gives an excellent idea of the sea bed around the cannon, but you must realize that this depicts only part of one small valley in

101

the reef. Other valleys, deeper and more mysterious, led away in all directions, their details becoming lost in the blue haze a hundred feet away. Toward the reef itself, the foaming water created a sparkling white fog—a deadly mist that surged up and down with every passing swell.

There was a lot of activity down there on the sea bed. Mike was chipping away with hammer and chisel at the half-exposed cannon while Peter was swimming along the wreck unrolling a tape measure. He was engaged in the very difficult but important operation of mapping the site.

To do this he had made a series of numbered tags, which he had stuck on the prominent objects such as the anchors and cannons. Then he measured the distances between them and noted the figures down on a sheet of plastic.

Nothing could sound easier, but listen to Peter's account of the operation:

I was continually getting tangled up with the tape. We built a kind of anchor at one end of it while I hung on to the other end, and I found that all the cannons seemed to be the same length. The measured length including the sea growth is eight to eight and a half feet. The variation is because I was getting washed around when I was making the measurements. . . . Where I was measuring, you can't even swim from one end of the site to the other. You have to hold on tight to the bottom while the opposing current runs by you, and then, when the current is

102

running your way, let go and be swept by the current to where you want to go and hold on when it stops. You have half a minute of lull, and then it sweeps the other way. I was banged all over. Once I caught my swim-fin in a crack in the rock, while I was being dragged in the opposite direction by the current, and thought my leg was being broken. . . . I lost my grip half a dozen times and once was swept twenty or thirty feet completely out of control, but I discovered that like everything else, this is something that you can get used to. Though it's very unpleasant and difficult, it is possible to work in that place. For instance, when I was swept, I just hunched over and made sure that my air bottle hit the coral cliff behind me. Mike said that he heard me going clang, clang, periodically as the seas crashed over the reef. . . .

Because I was very careful not to get far from the dinghy, I kept clear of this disturbed water, but even so the continual rise and fall of the swell presently brought on another mild attack of seasickness, so I got Laza to row me over to *Ran Muthu* while I flippered behind him, holding on to the dinghy with one hand. Then he hurried back to the divers while I relaxed, weak but very happy, on the deck of the boat. At least I had *seen* the site, and that made all the difference. The descriptions I had heard now began to make sense, and I could understand the problems that the divers were facing. It now seemed even more incredible to me that two years ago Mike and the

Divers returning to boat with finds.

two boys had been able to work here, at such a distance from their base on the lighthouse—*and* without a boat. They had been lucky enough to catch a brief spell of abnormally calm weather; otherwise their feat would have been quite impossible.

An hour later Peter and Mike rejoined me on the boat; Rodney, having taken a series of photographs with his Rolleimarine still camera, was paying a call on the lighthouse keepers—who seldom had visitors and were glad of the unexpected company.

"Well," I asked eagerly, "what about the treasure?"

The answer was disappointing.

"I think we got most of it last time," said Mike. "There doesn't seem to be much more."

Curiously enough, in a way I felt a certain relief. That meant the end of our main worries, as well as of hopes that we had never let ourselves take too seriously. Now at least we could turn our attention to some other project and leave this dangerous and exhausting work to the professional archaeologists like Peter, who seemed to thrive on it.

After hot cocoa and a few biscuits (in that blazing heat no one felt hungry, and it is unwise to eat much in the middle of a day's diving), Mike and Peter went back to the wreck. I decided not to run any more risks but to stay quietly on deck for the rest of the afternoon. My only regret was that, though I had seen the wreck, I had not actually reached it. Perhaps I should have put on an Aqua-Lung . . . but it was too late now.

Then, in the middle of the afternoon, the whole situation changed. We had now arranged a shuttle service with the two dinghies, one remaining always near the divers while the other ferried spare tanks and equipment between *Ran Muthu* and the site. Around 2 P.M. Peter came rowing back, and I am never likely to forget his first words to me: "I've found the mother lode. There's at least a ton there."

There was no need for explanations; I knew exactly what he meant.

10. The Bronze Cannon

Peter hurried back to the site with a spare Aqua-Lung cylinder, and I waited with what patience I could. A good hour passed, while the only sign of activity on the reef was Laza paddling back and forth, keeping an eye open for menacing swells. Then, at long last, I saw the two divers surface beside the dinghy, and it started to head back to *Ran Muthu*.

As it approached I saw that it was towing an extremely heavy load, partly supported in the water by an ingenious device that Peter had brought with him. This was the Port-A-Lift—a kind of underwater ballon which a diver can carry down in his pocket and inflate with air from his regulator.

The Port-A-Lift was sinking under the weight of a canvas sack, and it took the combined efforts of everyone on the boat to haul it over the side. I remember thinking, as I photographed the scene furiously, "I hope to goodness the sack doesn't tear open!" Then it *thunked* onto the deck, and Peter carefully lifted out the contents.

One by one, massive cylinders of lime-encrusted silver coins emerged from the sack. Each was about the same weight—roughly thirty pounds. Though they were so gray and corroded that no one would have noticed them if they had been lying in a rubbish heap, to us they looked beautiful. For we knew that beneath the protective outer layer of metal and coral the silver was still as clean and bright as the day it left the mint of Surat, when the Emperor Aurangzeb ruled two and a half centuries ago. Not that anyone would ever see it again, for these perfect thousand-coin masses were such rarities that it would be an archaeological crime to split them open. Probably nowhere else in the world—except for that one specimen we had donated to the Smithsonian and those still in the

The first four coin masses aboard Ran Muthu.

chest back in Colombo—did complete sacks of Mogul rupees exist, just as they had been sealed up in the counting house thirty years before George Washington was born.

That day's diving would have been enough to satisfy most people; but as long as there was any air left in the tanks, Mike and Peter weren't going home. So they returned to the site to continue digging away at the bronze cannon, while I brooded thoughtfully over those sausage-shaped lumps drying out in the sun.

Meanwhile Rodney had also had a successful afternoon,

bringing back a splendid thirty-five-pound red snapper, which would solve our food problems for the next couple of days. Treasure was all very well, but you could not eat it.

When we hauled up the anchor at 4 P.M. and started back for the mainland, we were all very happy. But now at last we were faced with the problem which, so far, had only been theoretical. Just what should we do with the treasure we had salvaged?

If we brought it ashore, under all those inquisitive eyes, there might be trouble. In any case, there was nowhere in the lighthouse shed where we could safely leave it. We decided—though this too involved some risks—that the best move would be to hide it under the tools and general junk in one of the obscurest of *Ran Muthu's* many lockers.

So that is what we did. We brought all the other finds ashore—ballast stones, cannon balls, the wooden plug of a grenade, the complete stock of a flintlock pistol—and made a great display of them to the evening audience.

As Peter dug and tapped his way through the lumps of coral he found one poignant relic—part of a lady's ear-ring, of a kind still seen in northern India to this day. It made the wreck come suddenly to life across the centuries, linking us to the unknown crew whose hopes and dreams had foundered with her.

Late that night, before settling down to a long and

Two fish wait hopefully for tidbits while Peter digs into the coral.
RODNEY JONKLAAS, B.SC.

undisturbed sleep beside the hull of the *Pharos II*, I went down to the beach to check that *Ran Muthu* was riding safely at anchor. The storm lantern lashed to her superstructure looked a very faint and distant star out there in the darkness, and it seemed most unlikely that anyone would row out, board her, force the padlock, and find the treasure hidden away inside her. The silver was safer there than on land—unless, by some irony of fate, *Ran Muthu* sank in the night and restored it once more to the bed of the Indian Ocean.

But she was still there in the morning when I walked down to the beach just before sunrise. Though Mike wanted me to come out again, I decided that this would be tempting Providence. Not only was I tired and sunburned after yesterday's exertions, but I had been suffering from agonizing and rather frightening cramps in my arms, hands, and neck. These were certainly due to the efforts my still partly paralyzed muscles had made when I was diving, clinging to the boat as she swayed in the water, and so on. They were probably a very good sign (if a muscle could hurt, I argued, it was trying to work again), but prudence demanded that I take a day's rest. Besides, there was shopping to do; Rodney's magnificent icebox was running out of ice.

So when *Ran Muthu* had set sail to the reef, Hector drove me to Hambantota, some thirty miles away. We were halfway back to Kirinda with our load of provisions and ice when the front suspension of the car collapsed and we ground noisily to the side of the road, scraping a long gouge across the tarmac. Luckily the car had chosen a good spot to break down; a few yards either way and it could have blocked the road completely.

Flagging lifts, finding a mechanic, hiring a truck, took several hours and most of our dwindling store of rupees (we sometimes wondered what the local tradesmen would say if we offered them Mogul ones, for we were nearly out of the modern variety). So it was after dark when we got back to Kirinda, and *Ran Muthu* had already returned. She had had another successful trip; for there, on the floor of the shed, was the beautiful bronze cannon I had seen the day before buried in the coral of the reef. It had taken two days' hard work to get it up with the help of an unusual underwater tool—an auto jack. Here is Peter's account of the operation, dictated into the tape recorder that same night:

The stern of the ship apparently went down where we've been working, and the central point of that area is the cannon that we managed to remove today. This area is quite obviously the lazeret of the ship, the stern part of the ship, which contains the powder room, the gun room, and the lazaret underneath the captain's cabin, where the money was usually stored in ships of this period. . . . Yesterday I began chipping through a concreted mass of hardened tar, gunpowder, the corrosion products of iron, all packed into a kind of stonelike material. . . . Nothing was lying in any special order, though included in the mess were musket barrels, the stock of a pistol, bits of iron, and hand grenades—hollow spheres of iron with the wooden plugs still in them. Going through this at the end of my dive, I noticed two sacks of silver concreted together. . . .

We decided that the cannon was lying right in the middle of all this gun room material, and it was essential to raise the cannon for two reasons. One, that rais-

ing it would loosen up all that material so that we could get under it and see if there were any more sacks of silver coins. And the second reason is that it's a conspicuous thing and marks the wreck. Obviously it's not advisable to leave a signpost there for somebody to see.

I worked getting scattered silver bits chipped off, chipping in the places where there seemed to be three or four rupees cemented together, and all the time working down under the cannon. Finally we had a place big enough so we could put in the jack; then I placed a heavy sledgehammer on a solid piece of rock under the breech of the cannon, and using a chisel as a wedge, began pounding it between the rock and the sledge while Mike levered with the auto jack. With those tons of pressure, the cannon broke loose, and we were very happy.

But chipping the cannon out of its coral tomb was only half the problem, even though it had taken the best part of two days. It had to be lifted onto *Ran Muthu*, which was several hundred feet away on the other side of a ridge of underwater hills.

This was where the Port-A-Life came in handy, but it could support only about a hundred pounds, and the cannon weighed at least three times as much. Here is Rodney's vivid account of the operation, which he photographed from all angles:

We had rather a hectic time getting the cannon off the

bottom. Mike was doing this with the aid of the Port-A-Lift, and we hitched both dinghies over the spot and tied three main ropes on the cannon. Peter very ably directed operations which enabled us to take the cannon a few feet off the bottom, where Mike could help us by pushing it over the rocks and reefs towards the sea. Once the ropes

The bronze cannon, freed from the coral with Port-a-Lift balloon.
RODNEY JONKLAAS, B.SC.

The bronze cannon goes up, guided by Mike.
RODNEY JONKLAAS, B.SC.

*were shortened considerably, we got the little outboard
motor started on one of the dinghies and chugged our
way, the cannon bumping along the bottom; but with
great luck we managed to get it over the various jagged*

boulders and reefs and out into deeper water, where, of course, the dinghy motor flatly refused to work from lack of fuel.

We then lowered the cannon to the bottom of the sea and left one dinghy on the spot. Then we went back to the boat in the other, feeling very happy. We had a lot of cocoa to drink, brought the Ran Muthu *back to the spot, anchored over it, and prepared to raise the cannon.*

This time I went down with an Aqua-Lung and managed to maneuver the cannon over a very tricky ledge. After that we tied two thick ropes on it, and after a great deal of heaving and hauling and pulling, we at last got the cannon into the boat. We felt quite relieved and happy and for the next hour or two were banging away at the cannon and cleaning it.

We spent a lot of time in the next few days breaking off the coral which formed a rocky crust over almost the entire surface of the cannon. The best way of getting rid of this was by straight hand bangs with a small hammer, being careful to hit only the coral, not the metal of the gun. Eventually the white lime would break up into powder and flake away; beneath it the gun was in almost perfect condition, showing no signs of corrosion or wear. It was hard to believe that it came from the same ship as the badly worn swivel guns that Mike had recovered on the earlier expedition.

Though we searched carefully, we found no crests, insignia, or other markings on the cannon which would tell us anything about her ownership. But we did discover, stamped around the breech, a series of numbers: 2 3 23 8. These Western numerals suggested that the gun was of European origin, and we hoped that they would tell an expert a great deal more than that. As you will see later, this hope was justified.

It had been a good day's work, marred only by three minor disasters. In addition to the car, dragged away to a local garage, both the underwater movie cameras were out of action—one probably for good. It had flooded on the first dive and was half full of water. When we unloaded the soggy mess hours later, the battery-driven motor was still running feebly. The other camera was not damaged, but its finder had been bent so that the operator could not tell what he was photographing. Ordinarily we would have been quite upset by these accidents, but we realized

*The bronze cannon after rough cleaning.
Scale in inches.*

that they were a small price to pay for what we had won from the sea. If we felt depressed, we had only to look at the beautiful cannon lying on the floor of the shed—or think of the silver tucked away inside *Ran Muthu.*

Not to mention the much larger amount still lying, we were sure, out there in that little valley on the reef.

11. Interlude, with Elephants

You may think it odd that, with a fortune in silver lying to be dug up, Mike and Peter spent at least half their time making maps and collecting old bronze cannons, wooden pistol stocks, rusty hand grenades, and similar items of no commercial value. But we were determined to act like scientists, not looters, and we wanted to learn everything that we could about this wreck. It was, after all, the first treasure ship ever found in the Indian Ocean, and it was our responsibility to see that the secrets it carried were not lost.

Moreover, there was a good practical reason for our behavior. If we could identify the ship, there was an excellent chance that we could discover her cargo. The Dutch and British merchants who were operating in this area at the beginning of the eighteenth century kept careful records of all their shipments, and most of these documents still exist in the various national archives, where research workers who know their way around can dig them out. A complete listing of this wreck's cargo, besides being of great interest, would be extremely invaluable to us. It would tell us what to look for and even *where*; for as Peter worked out the plan of the ship, he could deduce where the various items had been stowed. We would be particularly interested to know just how much silver she was carrying, so that we could tell what percentage we had already recovered.

The day after the cannon came ashore, we ran into bad luck. Perhaps I was the Jonah, for I had decided to go out and watch operations again. It was a lovely calm morning, perfect for diving; but only two miles out from Kirinda one of the engines seized up and stopped. The hot gases still leaking from the faulty exhaust appeared to be the cause of the trouble, and Mike decided that we could not continue operations until this had been repaired once and for all. So we turned back to Kirinda, ripped out the broken exhaust piping, and sat around gloomily looking at the mess and wondering what could be done.

There was nothing for it, Mike decided, but to drive back to Colombo with smoke-blackened bits and pieces and get a complete new set made. As the car was still under repair (we definitely seemed to be out of luck), we had to hire one locally. Mike and Hector departed at dusk, intending to drive through the night, and left the rest of us to hold the fort.

In some ways we did not mind the vacation, even though it was frustrating to think of the opportunities we were missing. There was plenty to do on land—checking equipment, making notes, photographing the finds. From time to time we would go down to the beach and look thoughtfully at the waves, wondering how long the sea would remain calm and how much time we would have left even if we could get *Ran Muthu* working properly again.

We took one evening off to drive into the great wild-life sanctuary of Yala, only twenty miles to the east of Kirinda. This is a huge area in which all hunting is forbidden; visitors are welcomed, but they must stay in their cars and be accompanied by an official guide. We drove slowly for about fifteen miles through narrow jungle roads, the guide telling us when to stop and pointing out sights of interest. There was one slightly anxious moment when a big bull elephant started walking purposefully towards us. Elephants usually ignore cars, but we did not stop to test this one's reactions. A little later we overtook a large black object shambling down the road ahead of us with a most peculiar walk; it was a bear, obviously more at home in the trees than on the level ground. We also saw boar, deer (one group forming a beautiful frieze against the edge of a lake as the sun went down behind them), and peacocks, as well as several more elephants. I was able to get a fine shot of one browsing in a forest glade. She looked so peaceful that I wished we could walk up and make friends, but this would not have been a good idea.

The holdup over the broken exhaust cost us three days of diving; it also cost us Rodney, who had to leave for an important and several-times-postponed underwater job up in the central mountains. This may seem an odd place to go diving, but it was in the artificial lake of a great hydroelectric project. Rodney's departure left us short of divers and threw a heavy load on Mike and Peter; however, he left his splendid icebox behind. He wouldn't need it up in the hills, where the temperature sometimes falls to a nippy 60°F.

Kirinda villagers listen to their tape-recorded songs.

When *Ran Muthu* finally set out again after her brief holiday, I remained on shore. The sea had been getting rougher during the last few days, and sometimes great waves would hit the rocky headland to the west of Kirinda and send curtains of spray shooting up into the air. This was not at all promising, and I feared that I had made my first and last visit to the reef this season.

While I was waiting for the boat to return that day, I persuaded some of the local youngsters to record their village songs, and the playbacks caused endless amusement. Having established a fund of good will with the tape recorder, I had no difficulty in getting volunteers to carry telescope, tripod, and cameras up to the top of the hill overlooking Kirinda. They were fascinated to see the lighthouse and passing ships brought from ten miles to within a few hundred yards, but I was much more interested in *Ran Muthu* as she bobbed up and down on the far side of the reef.

Visibility was remarkably good, despite the ten miles of hot, trembling air that lay between my hilltop and the reef. So I coupled the Nikon camera to the Questar, and shot off a roll of film. When I developed it back in Colombo, I was quite pleased with the result; *Ran Muthu's* canvas awning was clearly visible against the breakers foaming over the reef, with the white tower of the lighthouse looming in the background.

I watched from the hill for over an hour, swinging the telescope around the sky from time to time to look at the ships that were steaming past this busy crossroads in the sea. Then when I saw that *Ran Muthu* was bound for home, I went back to the lifeboat shed and told Anthony to get tea ready for the hungry divers.

Mike and Peter had spent most of the day learning more about the complicated geography of the wreck and had made some interesting discoveries. Peter had found a cannon no less than ten feet long; all the rest, except for our bronze one, were eight-footers. Mike had located a whole pile of ballast stones and had also discovered a fine copper serving plate, about sixteen inches in diameter, cemented into a mass of cannon balls and small chunks of coins. He worked for a long time to chip this plate loose but did not succeed.

He also found a bronze pestle (see page 94), in perfect condition, and spent some time looking for the mortar to go with it. But Mike never succeeded in completing the set; the mortar is still somewhere out there on the reef.

Copper serving plate from wreck (scale in centimeters).

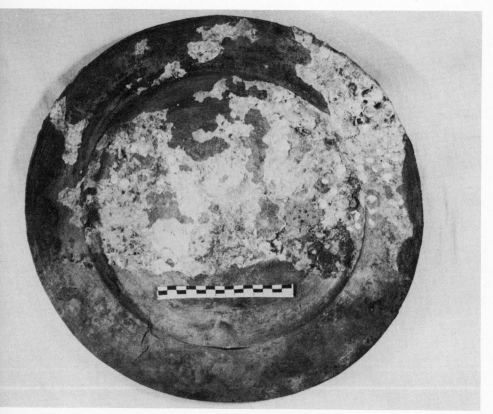

It was on this dive that Mike had his narrowest escape of the whole expedition, though he did not realize it until some hours later. He lost his hold in a sudden surge and was swept about twenty feet upward toward the surface. The abrupt and unexpected drop in pressure apparently strained his lungs, for that night he had a severe pain in his chest. We were all quite worried, but fortunately by next morning he was completely fit. If he had been swept upward a little more rapidly or had tried to hold his breath while the pressure around him suddenly dropped, he might well have been killed.

When I look back on this, the events of the next day cast certain doubts on my sanity. For despite Mike's unfortunate experience and everything that I had seen and heard, I let him talk me into going out to the reef again.

12. The Last Dive

We left late on the morning of April 21, for the fuel pump to one of the engines had failed and the temporary repairs had delayed us. There was no need to have bothered with them; even when Mike had fixed the fuel supply, the engine simply refused to turn over. It had completely seized up.

Despite this, and much against my better judgment, we went ahead on one engine, and by 10:30 were anchored a hundred yards off the reef. Conditions looked quite good, and this time I had no hesitation in putting on a single-tank Aqua-Lung and climbing—or rather falling—into the dinghy with Mike and Peter. Laza rowed us across to his usual parking site fifty feet from the wreck, and in we went.

I submerged very slowly, to give my ears plenty of time to adjust. (Eight years earlier I had punctured an eardrum on the Great Barrier Reef and have been very careful ever since.) Mike, who was keeping an eye on me, got the impression that I was not carrying enough weight to sink properly; so he swam over and handed me the four-pound hammer that he had been using to chip away the coral.

This took me down rather too fast, and I was so busy trying to blow my nose and clear my ears that I did not notice that the current was carrying me toward the reef. For suddenly, without any warning, I was seized by an irresistible force; I was absolutely helpless, as if in the grip of a giant hand.

The surge was swinging me back and forth—first towards the jagged, barnacled rocks of the reef, then away from them. Between each reversal of the current there were a few seconds while I hung motionless and had a chance to think; then I would be grabbed again as the tons of water started moving once more.

Only a few yards away I could see the wall of the reef rising like a cliff. Its highest levels, just below the rocking, mirror surface of the water, were almost hidden in a white mist of foaming bubbles—as the peaks of a mountain range may be shrouded by clouds. My great fear was that I would be swept up toward those peaks and over them into the seething water on top of the reef. Even a diver in good health would be badly knocked about—if nothing more—as he went over those rocks; in my condition, I was pretty sure I would have no chance at all.

I was almost equally worried about my Aqua-Lung mouthpiece, for it seemed that at any moment the surge would tear it from my teeth. I had to use my left hand to hold it in place, while my right was still frozen firmly onto the hammer that was inexorably pulling me down.

Unfortunately it was not pulling me down fast enough. I had hoped to descend into deeper, calmer water, but it was obvious that I was being dragged too swiftly toward the upper slopes of the reef. Now those deadly rocks, with their covering of razor-sharp barnacles, were only inches away, and I was smashing straight toward them.

There was only one thing to do, and I did it quite instinctively. I held out the hammer and let it take the shock of the impact. Then the pendulum swing of the surge swept me away again.

A second time I crashed against the rocks, still more violently. It was then—a little late, you may think—that I began to realize the seriousness of the situation. But I determined not to panic, for I knew that would be fatal. About three years earlier I had been caught in heavy surf off one of the Ceylon beaches and beaten down by the waves; Mike had got me out, at considerable risk to himself, with only seconds to spare. On that occasion I had felt the horrible, numbing fear that can drain all the strength from a man's limbs and all the reasoning power from his brain, turning him instantly into a terrified and helpless animal.

Holding out that hammer as a buffer, I fought simultaneously against the surge and against panic. I do not know how many more times the iron head of the hammer clanged against the reef—probably no more than two or three. Then I realized that my only hope lay in dropping the hammer, which was immobilizing my good arm, turning away from the reef, and swimming with all my strength out to sea.

I waited until I was at the greatest distance from the rocks, then released the hammer and swam for my life with hands and flippers. Luckily the dinghy was only a short distance away—it, too, seemed to have been dragged towards the reef—and I was able to reach it without difficulty. I clung thankfully to the trailing ropes, switched from Aqua-Lung to snorkel, and told Laza to tow me back to *Ran Muthu* as quickly as he could. I was not strong enough to climb into the dinghy and did not want to waste time taking off the Aqua-Lung in the water.

I was slightly, but only slightly, worried at leaving Mike and Peter, but they had seen me reach the safety of the dinghy, and when I last glimpsed them, they were already settling down to work as if these conditions were perfectly normal. As Laza rowed me away, I did have a sudden spasm of guilt; but it was definitely not because I was abandoning my colleagues to the mercy of the reef. I was worried in case I had lost the hammer, which was one of their most vital tools.

It seemed to take ages to get back to the boat, though I did my best to add a little speed with my flippers. The current toward the reef was obviously far stronger than it had been on any previous occasion; if it became any more powerful, I wondered if the divers would be able to make it back to *Ran Muthu*. I decided that when the dinghy returned to the reef, it would be at the end of a long nylon rope; then, whatever the strength of the current, we would be able to haul everyone back to the boat. Unless, of course, our own anchor dragged.

With Laza pushing and Martin pulling, I scrambled back aboard *Ran Muthu,* gouging a small valley in my shin in the process. As so often happens with wounds received in the sea, I felt nothing at the time; but now, months later, it is still an open sore which refuses to heal.

We tied the nylon line on the dinghy and sent Laza hurrying back to the reef while we played it out, making sure that there was no slack to get fouled in our propellors. All this seemed to take a very long time, and I began to get worried about Mike and Peter. Suppose, after all, they were in trouble?

To my vast relief I saw Mike surface just as the dinghy arrived off the reef and have a brief consultation with Laza. Then he went down again; obviously everything was under control.

I lay on the deck, slowly getting back my wind and my nerve, and wondering how the divers were faring. For the first time I really understood their difficulties, and my already considerable admiration for them went up several points. Yet at the same time I felt a little angry with them for getting me into such a dangerous situation in my semi-invalid state. They were aware of my limitations, so why had they let me dive?

It is easy to be wise after the event; I did not know, until we discussed the matter later, that the current had been almost as big a surprise to them as it was to me. But they had the strength—and the hard-won experience —to cope with it.

After two hours, while Laza bobbed around at the

end of the line, occasionally paddling briskly away from the reef when a big roller came along, Mike and Peter surfaced and climbed into the dinghy. When they got back to the boat, they had with them some small sacks of loose coins—and the fine brass tray or plate that Mike had been chipping away at for two days. Beneath its coral coating it was in excellent condition, apart from a few cracks that Mike had made as he levered it out of the reef.

After the usual biscuits and hot cocoa, the divers returned to the wreck. They thought my nylon line idea was a good one but modified it by fastening a float at its middle so that it would not sink down and get tangled round the rocks on the sea bed. So once again we had Laza bobbing around at the end of two hundred feet of nylon, a small satellite of *Ran Muthu*.

By this time I had fully recovered from the morning's fright and felt quite energetic again. I tossed a few pieces of paper into the water; they drifted away very slowly. The current had obviously slackened a good deal; conditions would be much better over on the reef.

Here was a challenge—a calculated risk. I thought it over for a while, then decided to accept it.

13. Farewell to the Reef

There was no danger, the way I had planned it. I put on face mask, flippers, weight belt—but no Aqua-Lung—gripped the snorkel in my teeth, and dropped over the side. Holding on to the nylon line with one hand, I swam and pulled myself slowly across to the dinghy. It was perfectly comfortable and perfectly safe, even though I was alone in the treacherous waters of the Great Basses.

The nylon line, about as thick as my little finger, had a breaking strain of many hundreds of pounds and was securely fastened to *Ran Muthu*. She in turn was held in place by twin anchors, so I felt completely confident as I worked my way over to the dinghy. Even though the current now seemed negligible, I took no chances. I never let go of the line but either gripped it or kept one arm hooked affectionately around it.

The afternoon had become cloudy, and with the dimming of the sun the underwater view was rather dull. There were no beautiful coral formations beneath me and not many fish. It was a drab no man's land of barnacled rocks and occasional pits and canyons.

Taking my time, I presently reached the dinghy and hovered underneath it, still holding on to the rope. Once again I peered down into that debris-filled little valley, which still held so many unknown treasures and secrets. Mike was hammering away at the base of a small cliff not far from the spot where the bronze cannon had rested. With this conspicuous signpost removed, the area was now just another uninteresting piece of sea bed. The scar of the underwater operation had already been filled by loose coral swept into it by the restless currents, which had even torn away some of the metal tags Peter had wired down as reference points for his map.

But where *was* Peter? I looked in all directions, up and down the valleys that stretched away into the distance. There was not the slightest sign of him; I could not even glimpse the regular bursts of silver bubbles which betray the presence of an Aqua-Lung diver. I was surprised but not particularly worried, for Mike was digging away with happy unconcern and presumably knew where Peter had gone.

Amateur and sports divers are always told to practice the "buddy" system—to remain in sight of each other and never to dive alone. This is excellent advice and should be obeyed—but not by professionals, who may sometimes have to break the rules to do a job of work. I was sure that Mike and Peter, with their thousands of hours of underwater experience, knew exactly what they were doing.

After hovering above Mike for about ten minutes, still clinging to the rubber boat, I became more adventurous. There was fifty feet of extra nylon rope on the dinghy, and I lashed one end around my waist, coiled up the rest in a few convenient loops, and cast adrift from my little floating island. I could now go swimming off in any direction, quite confident that I could pull myself back to the dinghy whenever I wished.

Mike was at a depth of about thirty feet, and I made several attempts to dive down to him. As might be expected, even my best efforts were pretty feeble; I was able to manage only about half the distance before having to turn back. As I passed the bottom of each dive, I hooted and shouted into the water, but Mike took not the slightest notice. I gave up trying to attract his attention and relaxed on the surface, watching his activities.

Presently he dropped the hammer and crowbar he had been using and started to swim away down the valley in a very purposeful manner. I guessed at once that he had found something interesting and was going to find Peter. Unreeling my safety line, I swam immediately above him (he still hadn't noticed me) and was not at all surprised when, at last, I saw a cloud of white bubbles ahead with the dim shape of Peter under them.

The two divers swam back to Mike's little corner of the reef, and there was an excited consultation on the sea bed. Then Peter came up to the dinghy and said, "Let me have a sack. Mike's found a couple of lumps as big as your head."

In the next five minutes I had a perfect bird's-eye view of the salvage operation, and I blessed my lucky stars that despite the morning's scare I had plucked up enough courage to come out to the reef again. For I was watching something which, I suppose, not more than a handful of living men have seen—the recovery of genuine treasure from the sea bed.

The sack that Peter had taken down had been tied onto

the end of my nylon line and was now resting on the sea bed. From time to time I gave it a tug; at first I was able to jerk it off the coral, but it became steadily heavier as work progressed. Before long I was barely able to budge it, and I decided to get closer to the scene of operations.

It is very much easier to pull yourself down into the sea, going hand over hand along a fixed line, than it is to swim. Every diver knows this and makes good use of convenient anchor chains as stairways. So this time I was able to get down to within a couple of yards of Mike and Peter. Even when I had hauled myself down the line, I had used so little energy and air that I was able to hover effortlessly over the reef for what semed enormous periods of time. (They probably did not exceed thirty seconds, but you can do and see a great deal in half a minute.) I remember thinking that I was probably the first diver in history who had used solid silver ballast to pull himself down to the sea bed.

Each time I dived I descended a little farther, and I would have touched bottom if the digging hadn't finished about then. It gave me a great feeling of satisfaction to know that I had come nearer to the wreck by my own lungpower (which twelve months earlier had been practically zero) than I had ever been able to do with an Aqua-Lung.

Peter and Mike got this consignment of silver free from

the reef with the last few breaths of air in their tanks. While they lifted it into the dinghy, I swam back ahead to alert Peiris, our photographer. We had intended to re-enact the recovery of the treasure, hauling some of the earlier lumps aboard *Ran Muthu* in front of the movie camera. But now there was no need for even this mild piece of cinematic faking. We were able to film the real thing at the moment it actually happened.

There was a great feeling of relaxation aboard the boat as we packed the gear for the return to Kirinda. We all knew that this was the last dive for this season—we would not risk going out again on one engine—and it could hardly have ended on a better note.

The two anchors came up for the last time from the cruel rocks of the Great Basses, the single engine started (to my relief), and we slowly drew out to sea. Mike did not take the shortest way home, even though it was getting late. Instead he took a swing round the lighthouse, passing very close to it and going right over the scene of our earlier expeditions.

The water had now become almost uncannily still; there was an oily calm, as if the reef was putting on its best behavior just to show what it could do when it felt like it. Beneath us I could see, wavering in the crystal water, the drowned caves and grottoes through which we had once swum with Ali Baba and Sinbad and Aladdin, and it was with a sense of sadness that we remembered they were no longer there.

The great granite tower of the lighthouse loomed above us, a tree of stone rooted so securely in rock that it had withstood the gales of almost a century. One of the light-keepers was standing on the lower platform, watching us as we chugged past—so close that we could have tossed a package of cigarettes across to him. "Good-by!" we called. "We'll be back next year!" Then we headed for Kirinda, ten miles away.

Halfway there, as I dozed on the foredeck, I was startled by a sudden explosion just behind me. Mike was blazing away with his Luger at a piece of floating wood. It was only his way of blowing off steam, but I wished he'd warned me. I was still very conscious of the fact that we were running on one engine.

We had never been out quite so late as this, for we had always been careful to return to our anchorage well before nightfall. The entry into Kirinda is tricky, owing to dangerous reefs and rocks, and is not to be attempted after dark. *Ran Muthu* was still several miles out; and ahead of us now was one of the most spectacular sunsets I have ever seen.

Miles inland, the sky was overcast by the black clouds of a heavy rainstorm. But its center was clear, and in this we could see the misty mountains that bear the name of one of Ceylon's most sacred places, the shrine of Kataragama. They were perfectly framed by the surrounding clouds, and the sun was going down behind them, painting them in such mysterious golds and purples that it was hard to believe that they were real. No theatrical designer could have contrived a more splendid stage setting; we seemed to be looking straight into the heart of fairyland. And I found myself thinking, as the light slowly faded from the western sky, that the beauty ahead of us was no illusion, no mere trick of sun and cloud. It was real, and we were returning to it, with our cargo of hard-won treasure.

14. The Monsoon

So ended, on a smooth, calm sea, the greatest adventure
of my life. But the story of this wreck has barely started
to unfold; it is going to keep us busy for many years to
come.

When we got back to Colombo, we settled down to

Elizabeth shows Tony Wilson ten times his own weight in silver. This photograph shows all the specie recovered by the 1961 and 1963 expeditions, except for the mass donated to the Smithsonian.

examine and to photograph our finds, and Peter Throck-morton (who had to fly back to Athens in a few days) taught us how to preserve them. Wooden and iron objects brought up out of the sea, after a few centuries under-water, soon crumble to pieces unless they are properly treated.

It was a busy and anxious time, for *Ran Muthu,* with an engine out of action, was still anchored at Kirinda, and we did not know how long the lull before the monsoon would last. But Martin and Laza got her back safely to

144

Colombo a few days later, though some kind persons had cut the anchor chain, presumably in the hope that she would go aground, and there had been an attempt to steal one engine.

We had consultations with lawyers and government officials over the disposal of the treasure and made arrangements to display our finds at the Colombo Museum. We also made one very interesting discovery about the bronze cannon that Mike and Peter had chipped out of the sea bed.

I have already mentioned the numbers marked on the breech—2 3 23 8. When we wrote to the Smithsonian Institution and asked Mendel Peterson what this meant, he answered that it was the English way of indicating the weight of a gun. The "2" would be hundredweight, the "3" quarter-hundredweights, and the "23" the odd pounds. The final "8" was simply the number of the gun. Allowing for the fact that in the peculiar English system of measures a hundredweight is 112 pounds, this would add up to 331 pounds.

We took the gun around to the nearest heavy-duty scale and heaved it into the platform. It weighed 332 pounds. The few patches of coral were enough to account for the difference.

The gun therefore was English, so perhaps the ship belonged to the *British*—not, as we had first assumed, to the *Dutch*—East India Company. But a single gun proves little, and much more evidence is needed. We hope that the researchers we have at work in the libraries and archives of several countries will find it.

And what of the treasure? Some three hundred pounds of it are sharing my office with me at the moment. The rest—much the greater part, we are sure—is still out there on the reef.

It is perfectly safe where it is. Soon after *Ran Muthu* had chugged back into the shelter of Colombo Harbor, the southwest monsoon began to show its strength. Violent gusts of wind swept across the city, overturning trees, scattering leaves and branches in all directions. Rain fell in torrents; within a few hours, the roads over which we

The Little Basses lighthouse. What wrecks remain to be discovered in this completely unexplored territory? ROYAL CEYLON AIR FORCE

had driven back from Kirinda were feet deep in water—or even swept completely away.

Out on the reef tremendous breakers are now pounding against the base of the lighthouse, shooting clouds of spray far up the granite tower. Shark's Tooth Rock must be hidden beneath foam boiling and seething around it; no boat could possibly get near the site of the wreck without being dashed to pieces. Conditions will remain that way for almost a year; and then, perhaps, we may return, with a larger boat and better equipment.

Or perhaps not. We have learned that there is no great hurry in the sea. We have taken steps to safeguard the site and to discourage unauthorized visitors. If we go back two years or ten years from now, we will find things just as we left them, with the rest of the silver still intact in our private vault.

The treasure has been there for 260 years. It can wait a little longer.

Format by The Etheredges
Set in Intertype Garamond
Composed by The Haddon Craftsmen, Inc.
Printed by The Murray Printing Company
Bound by The Haddon Bindery
Harper & Row, Publishers, Incorporated